Made to Create
with All My Heart
and Soul

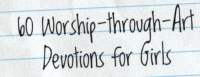
60 Worship-through-Art
Devotions for Girls

made to
CREATE

with all my heart and soul

written & illustrated by
Lauren Duncan

Tyndale House Publishers, Inc.
Carol Stream, Illinois

Visit Tyndale online at www.tyndale.com.

Visit Lauren Duncan online at www.laurenjohnstonduncan.com.

TYNDALE and Tyndale's quill logo are registered trademarks of Tyndale House Publishers, Inc.

Made to Create with All My Heart and Soul: 60 Worship-through-Art Devotions for Girls

Designed by Jacqueline L. Nuñez

Edited by Sarah Rubio

Published in association with the literary agency of Legacy, LLC, 501 N. Orlando Avenue, Suite #313-348, Winter Park, FL 32789.

For manufacturing information regarding this product, please call 1-800-323-9400.

For information about special discounts for bulk purchases, please contact Tyndale House Publishers at csresponse@tyndale.com, or call 1-800-323-9400.

ISBN 978-1-4964-3127-1

Printed in China

25	24	23	22	21	20	19
7	6	5	4	3	2	1

This book is dedicated to all the uniquely beautiful and wonderfully created girls God has placed in my life—some for a season, some all grown up already, some who I hope will read this years from now—especially the "still littles" of the bunch: Mackenzie, Clara Hayes, Josephine, and Dorry Ann.

Contents

Introduction

Before you dive into this book, I have a little challenge to get you ready! It might seem strange or hard, but trust me, there is a point to this. I promise it will be worth it!

Here goes: draw a rose from memory below. Yeah—right now. Go!

ART NOTE

Subject Matter: The topic, feeling, or object represented in a work of art.

Now copy the picture of the rose above by drawing *what you see*. Pretend you have NO idea what it is—just focus on the shapes, lines, and textures.

Now let me guess—the second drawing is a lot more realistic, right? Here's the connection: if you want to draw a real-looking flower, you need to look at real flowers. You need to spend time studying them, looking at them from every angle. That's how you learn the truth of how flowers look and are put together. Then you respond to that truth by drawing what you've seen— over and over and over! In the same way, if we want to grow as followers of Christ, we must do these three things:

1. Seek for and look at the truth.
2. Study the truth.
3. Respond to the truth.

That's going to be our goal as we go through this study together!

Don't copy the behavior and customs of this world, but let God transform you into a new person by changing the way you think. Then you will learn to know God's will for you, which is good and pleasing and perfect.

Romans 12:2

Let's leave behind what we think we know and start seeking the TRUTH, even if it's not exactly what we thought it was. Let's get real, dig deep, and create!

Created with Purpose

I praise you because I am fearfully and wonderfully made;
your works are wonderful, I know that full well.
Psalm 139:14, NIV

Every Christian is to become a little Christ.
The whole purpose of becoming a Christian is
simply nothing else.
C. S. Lewis

Day 1

I praise you because I am fearfully and wonderfully made; your works are wonderful, I know that full well.

Psalm 139:14, NIV

Have you ever been told how precious you are? If you're anything like me, you have days when you believe it and days when you don't. I'm writing this book to show you just how true it is! We may not have met in person yet, but I already know you are wonderfully created!

Are you ready for your first bit of evidence? God says so! Look at the verse above, then fill in the blanks below:

I am _____ and

_____ made!

Now look at the rest of the verse. What does the writer of this psalm (who happens to be King David) say next?

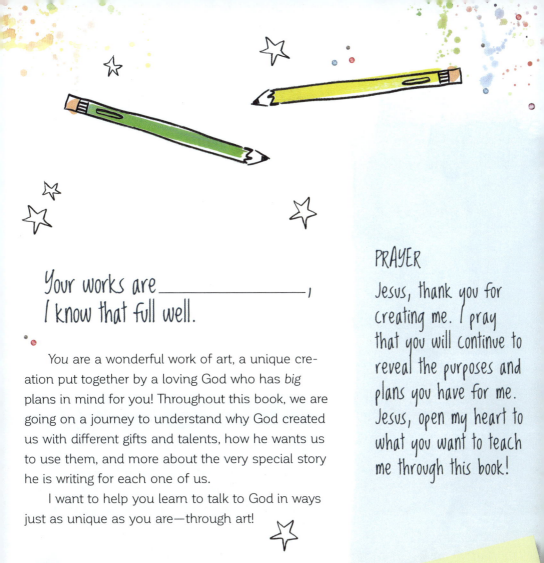

Your works are _____,
I know that full well.

You are a wonderful work of art, a unique creation put together by a loving God who has *big* plans in mind for you! Throughout this book, we are going on a journey to understand why God created us with different gifts and talents, how he wants us to use them, and more about the very special story he is writing for each one of us.

I want to help you learn to talk to God in ways just as unique as you are—through art!

PRAYER

Jesus, thank you for creating me. I pray that you will continue to reveal the purposes and plans you have for me. Jesus, open my heart to what you want to teach me through this book!

You are fearfully & wonderfully made. = You are pretty SPECIAL!

BIBLE JOURNAL

SUPPLY LIST

- box (shoe box, tissue box, or any other empty box you can find)

- scissors

- butcher paper, kraft paper, or brown paper bag

- tape

- permanent marker

- paint, markers, colored pencils, crayons, or anything else you want to color with

- paintbrush (if using paint)

- cup of water (if using paint)

- stickers, glitter, ribbons, sequins, or anything else you want to use to decorate your box

- glue

OVERVIEW

We are going to start with Scripture memory. The verse at the beginning of each chapter is going to be our verse for the week. Each week you're going to create a beautiful card with our verse written on it. You can use the card throughout the week to help you memorize the verse—read it through several times each day, until you can say it without looking. But first, you need to make a box to keep all your verse cards in!

STEPS

1. Cover your box and lid separately with brown paper. Fold in the corners like you're wrapping a gift and tape them down.
2. Write this week's verse on the box with a permanent marker. If you want, you can write key words that stand out to you in a different color or style (like bubble letters; see the Lettering Art Note on page 20 and the Bubble Letters Art Note on page 42).
3. Use the supplies you've gathered to decorate your box and make it beautiful!

Day 2

You have searched me, LORD, and you know me. You know when I sit and when I rise; you perceive my thoughts from afar.
Psalm 139:1-2, NIV

Well, hey there. I was just too excited yesterday and jumped right in without introducing myself! My name is Lauren Duncan, and I'm a longtime art teacher and an even-longer-time follower of Jesus! I love to bake chocolate chip cookies and plant flowers in my garden. I really love to paint my prayers! My days on earth have been full of good and bad, joy and hurt, peace and loneliness—and our good God created me with special gifts to face each of those days. Each of our stories looks different, so we all require different gifts.

Let's open our Bibles back up to Psalm 139. Today we're going back to the beginning of the chapter.

Did you realize that God knows our thoughts? Today's verse says God has searched us and that he *knows* us. That's sort of good and sort of bad, right? I kind of wish God would just know all the good things about me and not have to know the bad stuff. But the Bible says that he knows everything. And we know from yesterday's verse that he thinks we are wonderful . . . even still! So you can feel safe talking to him about the bad stuff, especially since he knows about it already. And guess what? He is the one who has the power to heal and change it.

Today, I want you to start a conversation with God about the things that make you happy and the things that make you sad, angry, or scared. You can write it out or say it out loud. Before you start, take a few seconds to remember that he already knows all about it:

Before a word is on my tongue you, LORD, know it completely. You hem me in behind and before, and you lay your hand upon me.
Psalm 139:4-5, NIV

Just talk to him, and then let these words wash over you:

The LORD replied, "I have forgiven them, as you asked."
Numbers 14:20, NIV

PRAYER

Jesus, thank you for knowing me so well that you know what I'm going to say before I even say it! Thank you, Jesus, for listening to me and offering me your forgiveness. Please go before me today and help me learn more about you.

BIBLE JOURNAL

SUPPLY LIST

- mirror (freestanding or wall hanging, but large enough to see most of your body)
- sketchbook or piece of paper
- pencils, pens, markers, or whatever you like to draw with

OVERVIEW

Use a sketchbook as your Bible journal for the art projects in this book (except for the weekly verse cards). If you don't have a sketchbook, do the activities on loose pieces of paper and keep them all together in a box or folder.

Today, we are going to spend some time thinking about how God loves all of our unique gifts, interests, fears, and thoughts. Look up Luke 12:7 if you need some encouragement!

STEPS

1. Find a mirror that you can see your reflection in and sit and draw comfortably at the same time.
2. Look yourself in the eye and say the verses from today and yesterday out loud.
3. Draw a contour line (like tracing around a shadow) of your basic shape, taking up most of the paper. Don't worry about details at all—it can be a single line that may include just your torso and head or your whole body, depending on the size of your mirror.
4. Draw a vertical line straight down the center of your page (from top to bottom).
5. On the right side of this line, inside your outline, write or draw all the things that bring you joy.
6. On the left side, inside your outline, write or draw all the things that make you sad, angry, or scared.
7. Last, write the verses from today (Psalm 139:1-2) around your outline.

If you are doing this book with a small group, this activity is a great way to get to know each other!

ART NOTES

Picture Plane: A two-dimensional (2-D) space perpendicular to the viewer's sight (represented by your canvas or paper).

Composition: How all the individual pieces or elements are arranged in a work of art.

Elements of Art: Individual pieces or components that can be used to create a work of art.

Day 3

The Lord said to Moses, "See, I have chosen Bezalel son of Uri, the son of Hur, of the tribe of Judah, and I have filled him with the Spirit of God, with wisdom, with understanding, with knowledge and with all kinds of skills—to make artistic designs for work in gold, silver and bronze, to cut and set stones, to work in wood, and to engage in all kinds of crafts.

Exodus 31:1-5, NIV

How stinkin' cool is it that God has given us all superspecial gifts? Can you believe that in the Old Testament he gave someone the gift to "engage in all kinds of crafts"? At school, it can be easy to get bummed out when others make the best grades or have the coolest clothes or get picked first in PE class . . . but our God is so much bigger than that! And I'll say it again—he made *you* with a very special purpose!

On the next page, rewrite today's verses, filling in your name and some of your gifts. If you can't think of any of your gifts, ask your friends or family, or ask your adult to help you find a spiritual gifting test online.

The Lord said to Moses, "See, I have chosen _____, daughter of _____, from the city of _____, and I have filled her with the Spirit of God, with wisdom, with understanding, with knowledge and with all kinds of skills—to:

1. _____

2. _____

3. _____

Take time to praise Jesus for the specific gifts that you listed above, the gifts that he has given to you, his wonderfully created daughter.

PRAYER

Jesus, I thank you for creating me with unique talents and skills! I pray that you would bless the work of my hands as I learn to glorify you through them.

BIBLE JOURNAL

SUPPLY LIST

- ultrasound or baby picture of YOU
- sketchbook or piece of paper
- pencil
- watercolor paint
- small paintbrush
- cup of water

OVERVIEW

Today we are going to take time to reflect on how God knit each one of us together!

STEPS

1. Look at your picture and find all the lines and shapes that make you! (Probably lots of different ovals for your head, body, arms, and legs.)
2. Draw the same basic shapes and lines in your sketchbook or on a piece of paper.
3. Dip the paintbrush in the water and paint inside your shapes with water.
4. Dip the paintbrush in one color of watercolor paint. Add a dot of the color to the water inside your drawing.
5. Rinse your paintbrush, then add a dot of a different color to your painting. Repeat until you have a dot of each color. Notice how the colors bleed and blend together. Think about how God knit *you* together in the womb—think about how amazing you are!
6. If you want, ask your adult to tell you some stories about the time when they were waiting for you to come or when they first met you! Write some of these stories around your painting.

ART NOTES

Line: The space between two points. Lines can be horizontal, diagonal, vertical, wavy, looped, dotted, zigzag, etc.

Shape: An enclosed two-dimensional (2-D) space, often defined by a line.

Organic Shapes: Shapes that do not follow rules; they are often asymmetrical (not even on both sides). Shapes found in nature are usually organic.

Geometric Shapes: Shapes that follow rules (for example, math shapes such as circles, squares, triangles, rectangles, or ovals).

Day 4

> He raised us from the dead along with Christ and seated us with him in the heavenly realms because we are united with Christ Jesus.
> Ephesians 2:6

Yesterday, we learned about the unique gifts God has given us. Today I want to look at the *purpose* of these gifts! Let's read some verses that follow today's Scripture:

> God can point to us in all future ages as examples of the incredible wealth of his grace and kindness toward us, as shown in all he has done for us who are united with Christ Jesus. . . . For we are God's masterpiece. He has created us anew in Christ Jesus, so we can do the good things he planned for us long ago.
> Ephesians 2:7, 10

So, God has created us to know Christ (verse 6), to be an example to others (verse 7), and to do _____ things he planned for us long ago (verse 10). And it also says (this is my favorite part!): "for we are God's _____."

Wait, whaaa?! Who is God's masterpiece? Yes! It's you. And what is the purpose of a masterpiece? Think about it for a minute: Why would you take the time to create something?

_____

_____

_____

_____

I take my time creating artwork to reflect God's glory and to beautify our world. Dictionary.com says a masterpiece is "a person's greatest piece of work" and an "example of skill or excellence."

The unique gifts and talents God has given us are to display his glory—to point others to him!

Now, go back to the beginning of today's lesson and read the verse again. Circle which words are used:

He will raise	He is in the process of raising
He might raise	He raised

You got it! He has already prepared us to be his masterpiece! I remember the moment the Lord put a call on my heart to be in ministry. I was so excited! I knew he was going to send me to Africa—so what did I do? I sat down and started making plans, of course! I changed my college major to pre-med (because God needs medical missionaries) and started "raising myself up" for his purpose. What happened, you ask? I failed chemistry class because I wasn't using the gifts God had blessed me with. When I let God do the "raising" and started using the gifts and talents he had given me, the Lord raised me up for his purpose in ministry! I got to use my gifts to serve at an international Christian school in West Africa, teaching art to kids from all over the world. And now, I get to minister to you! How amazing God's plans for us are!

PRAYER

Jesus, raise me up for your purposes! Please show me my gifts so I can use them to glorify you. I pray that you would make a way for me to proclaim your name in all the earth!

BIBLE JOURNAL

SUPPLY LIST

- sketchbook or piece of paper
- pencil (a number 2 pencil is great, but if you want a different one, the softer the better)
- paper towel or tissue
- small printed picture of yourself (optional)
- tape (optional)

Value: The lightness or darkness of a color.

Tint: A color plus white.

Tone: A color plus gray.

Shade: A color plus black.

ART NOTES

OVERVIEW

Today's project is all about remembering that God's got this! We were fearfully and wonderfully made to do things he planned for us!

STEPS

1. Find a hand model—it can be your own hand or someone else who is willing to sit still long enough for you to draw their hand. Turn the hand palm up, like it's holding something up.
2. Practice drawing as lightly as you possibly can with your pencil in the corner of your paper.
3. Now, starting with the wrist, draw the outline of the hand, still as lightly as you can.
4. Go back and add details, like the fingernails and wrinkles. Remember, you're still drawing super lightly!
5. Now, add value (lights and darks) to create shadows and highlights. You can slant your pencil so the edge of the sharpened point is at an angle to your paper. This will allow you to get a medium to light value. To create darker values, use the tip of your sharpened pencil and press a little harder. The darker values should be shadows on the bottom of your hand and the lighter values should be on top where the light is hitting.
6. Rub the shaded areas gently with the tissue or paper towel to blend the shadows. This will make any hard edges softer.
7. Last, draw a tiny YOU or tape a small printed picture of yourself inside the hand like it's holding you up!

If you want to, you can add today's verse to your drawing anywhere you like!

Form: A three-dimensional (3-D) space; a shape that has height, width, and depth (for example, cubes, pyramids, spheres, or cylinders). These shapes block light, creating a range of values and shadows on and around them.

Day 5

This is the written account of Adam's family line. When God created mankind, he made them in the likeness of God.

Genesis 5:1, NIV

The LORD said to Moses, "Come up to me on the mountain and stay here, and I will give you the tablets of stone with the law and commandments I have written for their instruction."

Exodus 24:12, NIV

Let this be written for a future generation, that a people not yet created may praise the LORD.

Psalm 102:18, NIV

Jesus said to him, "Away from me, Satan! For it is written: 'Worship the Lord your God, and serve him only.'"

Matthew 4:10, NIV

Read the above passages and circle the word **written** in each one. These are all powerful verses that refer to God's Word being written truth. There must be something to this! God's Word is full of the handwritten letters of apostles and prophets—witnesses to God's work. If writing letters and recording what God is doing was part of all these people's lives, why wouldn't we do it too?

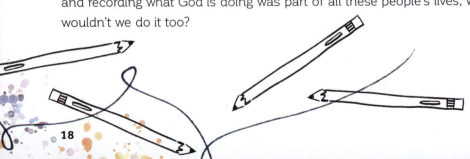

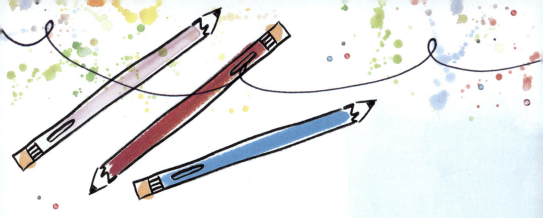

In these four passages the written account was for various purposes:

1. Genesis 5:1—To record _____ _____

2. Exodus 24:12—For God to give his _____ _____

3. Psalm 102:18—For future _____ to read (that's you!)

4. Matthew 4:10—To protect us from _____

Wow! Those are four good reasons to read what was written for us, to study it, and to memorize it! Let's start reading God's Word and writing what God is doing in our lives today!

PRAYER

Jesus, I thank you for your written Word! I thank you for writing it for me to learn from and to find protection in. Please show me how to record what you are doing in my heart, for my good and for the good of others!

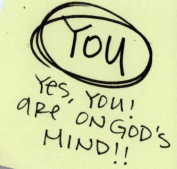

YOU

YES, YOU! are ON GOD'S MIND!!

BIBLE JOURNAL
weekend challenge

Lettering: The art of drawing letters. This is different from calligraphy in that the letters are "drawn" as opposed to "written."

ART NOTE

OVERVIEW

I am sooooo excited about our first weekend challenge! We are going to explore hand lettering! I am going to show you a few ideas I have to get you started. You may have played with different fonts on a computer—hand lettering is similar in that you can communicate feelings and ideas with HOW you write something.

STEPS

1. Look at the Lettering Art Note for some ideas.
2. Come up with a theme for your unique letters! It can be based on something you like to do or eat, lines you like to draw, fonts you like to use when typing, or anything that inspires you. Even your pet!
3. Write out the alphabet in big block letters really lightly with your pencil.
4. Go back and try to add something from your theme to make each letter fun and unique. Take your time! Remember, you have all weekend to do this—so play around and have some fun with it!

ART NOTES

Typography: The study of how to arrange letters and words artistically.

Font: A set of letters and numbers sharing similar characteristics..

A serif font has a small line attached to each letter or brush stroke:

This is a serif font.
This also is.
And this one too.

A sans serif font does not have these. My favorite sans serif font is Century Gothic because it looks so clean. **This is another example of a sans serif font.** The most popular sans serif font is called Helvetica—there's a whole documentary about it!

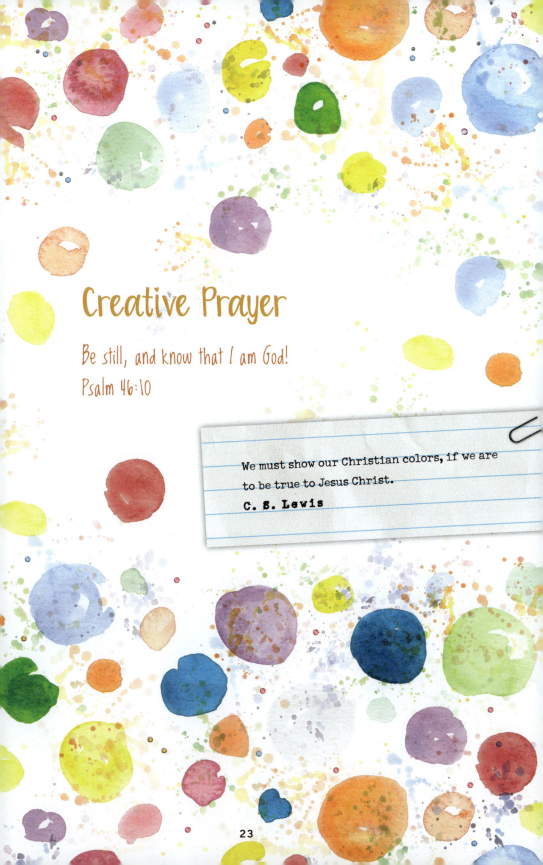

Creative Prayer

Be still, and know that I am God!
Psalm 46:10

We must show our Christian colors, if we are to be true to Jesus Christ.

C. S. Lewis

Day 1

Be still, and know that I am God!
Psalm 46:10

Hey, hey! The verse this week is about *how* we come before the Lord in prayer. Before we even begin to speak to God, it's important to have our hearts in the right posture. "What does that mean?" you ask . . .

According to the dictionary (Merriam-Webster's, to be exact), the first definition of *posture* is "the position or bearing of the body whether characteristic or assumed for a special purpose."

The physical postures that a lot of people connect with prayer (kneeling, eyes closed, hands together) can seem silly. Do we kneel just because that's how we were taught, and how our mamas' mamas were taught? Why do we hold our hands that way? And do we *really* have to close our eyes? (My mom used to get so mad when we kids would peek during the blessing at dinner!)

Taking this to God's written Word, I can't find any place where we are taught to close our eyes! In fact, we see almost the opposite of this when King Nebuchadnezzar "raised [his] eyes toward heaven, and [his] sanity was restored" (Daniel 4:34, NIV). I found a dozen places where people pray with their hands raised ("spread out his hands toward heaven," 1 Kings 8:22, NIV) and/or kneeling down ("let us kneel before the LORD our Maker," Psalm 95:6-7, NIV). Have you ever read John's reaction to seeing God for the first time? He says, "When I saw him, I fell at his feet as though dead" (Revelation 1:17, NIV).

What?! He saw God and fell down?! This verse reminds me of the force of a wave at the beach, or a wind so powerful that it could knock you down. How much more powerful is God than the wind and waves?

Let's look at another definition of *posture* from the very same dictionary: "a conscious mental or outward behavioral attitude." That's the posture I'm talking about! Prayer isn't about our physical posture as much as our spiritual posture. If we take a minute to remind ourselves of who God is, a tidal wave of love should bring us to our spiritual knees. Whether you are sitting, standing, dancing, jogging, or in class with your eyes wide open, what matters is the posture of your heart. The reason people sometimes physically get on their knees or close their eyes to pray is that it helps them get their hearts in the right position. So before you pray, take a moment to find a physical posture that helps you to be still and KNOW that HE is God.

PRAYER
Father God, thank you for being a God I can call on anytime. Thank you for being all powerful and still having time to talk with me. I ask that you continue to remind me to quiet my heart before I come to you, Creator of all!

BIBLE JOURNAL

SUPPLY LIST

- cardboard (an empty cereal box or a packing box)
- ruler
- scissors
- aluminum foil
- tape
- dull pencil

OVERVIEW

This week we're going to write our memory verse on a surface that is smooth and reflective like a still pond.

STEPS

1. Cut a piece of cardboard to index-card size (3 inches by 5 inches).
2. Cut a piece of aluminum foil a few inches bigger than the cardboard piece.
3. Cover the cardboard with the aluminum foil, being careful to keep the front side as smooth as possible. Fold the edges over and tape them down on the back side of the card.
4. Flip the card over to the front side and "carve" this week's verse into the card with your dull pencil.

Day 2

Accept my prayer as incense offered to you, and my upraised hands as an evening offering.

Psalm 141:2

Have you ever burned incense before? Let's just say I had a phase. . . . Now I like to burn candles in my home. It helps when we forget to take the trash out or come home sweaty from the gym. But one time, we had a terrible smell in our house that we could NOT get out! We lit candles, sprayed air fresheners, took the trash out again and again, cleaned all our corners and even under the bed . . . and the smell just kept getting worse! Finally my husband nervously said, "It has to be something under the house." Oh dear. A few hours later, we had retrieved the biggest, most disgusting, WORST-smelling dead opossum from under our house!

The point: we couldn't cover up the stink without dealing with the actual problem. We had to

1. recognize the stink,
2. clean it up, and
3. begin the good smells again.

If we want our prayers to be incense to God, we need to smell ourselves first. We have to clean up before we start with the good smells! So how do we clean up so we can get to the good stuff?

I acknowledged my sin to you and did not cover up my iniquity. I said, "I will confess my transgressions to the LORD." And you forgave the guilt of my sin.
Psalm 32:5, NIV

In your prayer time, it's important to be real with God. Ask him what you need to clean out. If you're trying to cover up an opossum with incense, God's going to smell the stink. Make sure you are talking with God about all that is going on, dealing with the truth, and asking him for help!

If you haven't ever confessed that you need help with the big stink of sin in your life, and if you feel led to pray and ask Jesus into your heart, I would love to lead you in that prayer: "Lord, I confess I am in need of a savior, and that savior is Jesus Christ. Please forgive me for my sins and help me turn away from them. I ask you to send your Holy Spirit into my heart to change me and allow me to have a personal relationship with you."

PRAYER
God, I praise you for knowing the truth! I ask, Lord, that you would help me see where I stink, so I can confess and clean up and my prayers can be a beautiful fragrance for you.

GRACE
GRACE
GRACE

BIBLE JOURNAL

SUPPLY LIST

- a pitcher of water
- several plastic cups
- dish soap
- paint, dye, or markers (old ones that it's time to upcycle)
- drinking straw
- sketchbook or piece of paper
- pencils, pens, markers, or whatever you like to draw with

OVERVIEW

Today we are going to imagine and illustrate how our prayers might look rising up to heaven! This may be messy, so ask the adult in charge where to create today!

STEPS

1. Fill a cup halfway with water and add a drop of dish soap (just a little will do!).
2. Now drop in a dollop of paint or dye, or take the lid off an old marker and let it soak in the cup for a minute, until the water starts to change color.
3. Take a straw and blow into the cup (not too hard and not too soft, just like Goldilocks) until you see colorful bubbles rise to the top of your cup.
4. Take your sketchbook or another piece of paper and set it on top of the cup to create a print of the bubble pattern.
5. Repeat these steps as many times as you like. Try adding different colors of paint to the water. Think about how the color you add changes what rises up.
6. Use pencils, pens, or markers to add details to your art—maybe one cluster of bubble art becomes a flower!

Day 3

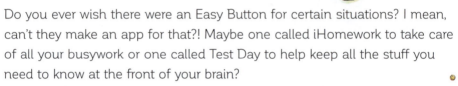

Know that the LORD, he is God! It is he who made us, and we are his; we are his people, and the sheep of his pasture.
Psalm 100:3, ESV

Do you ever wish there were an Easy Button for certain situations? I mean, can't they make an app for that?! Maybe one called iHomework to take care of all your busywork or one called Test Day to help keep all the stuff you need to know at the front of your brain?

When I am praying, sometimes I just wish there was an iPray app that could tell me exactly what to say. A perfect recipe to get a yes from God, or a magic spell to just make a hard situation go away. I do NOT want to have to deal with making up with my sisters, or telling my mom I'm sorry! Can't I just say a few "right" words and have it all fixed? And then I read this verse:

We are God's handiwork, created in Christ Jesus to do good works, which God prepared in advance for us to do.
Ephesians 2:10, NIV

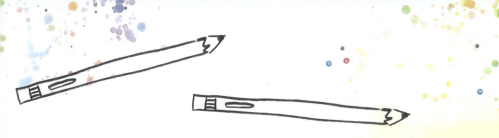

This verse says that God created us to do "_____ works," which he "prepared in _____ for us to do." If he already knows what we are going to pray or say and what's going to happen in the end, what's the point in praying at all? Easy Button, please!

The point is a relationship. God has created us for good works, and because he wants to have a relationship with us, we are "his people" (Psalm 100:3, ESV).

God so loved the world that he gave his one and only Son, that whoever believes in him shall not perish but have eternal life.

John 3:16, NIV

Prayer is NOT about just learning the right words to say. It's about more than getting the results you want. It's about getting to know your Creator.

PRAYER
Father God, thank you for creating me for good. Please remind me that our relationship is not about getting what I want, but about getting to know YOU.

BIBLE JOURNAL

OVERVIEW

Today, we are trying to approach a blank piece of paper the same way we come to God in prayer—looking, asking, responding to what happens along the way. A relationship with God through prayer is a lot like a "process-based" painting. This is the opposite of a "product-based" painting, where the artist decides exactly what and how she wants to paint before she even gets started. Jackson Pollock is one of my favorite process painters. He would play with his paint and add brushstrokes until he felt a piece was complete. To do this kind of painting, we need to meet the paper with no plan. No color scheme. No subject matter. Don't worry a bit about what your art will look like—just play!

STEPS

1. Spread out your drop cloth outside or in an area of your house where it's okay to get messy.
2. Set your sketchbook or piece of paper on top of the drop cloth.
3. PRAY! Ask God to help you to listen and be open to what he is doing in all areas of your life.
4. Throw or sling paint onto the paper with your stick and paintbrush until your piece feels finished to you.

Day 4

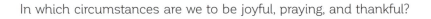

*Always be joyful. Never stop praying.
Be thankful in all circumstances, for this is
God's will for you who belong to Christ Jesus.
1 Thessalonians 5:16–18*

In which circumstances are we to be joyful, praying, and thankful?

_____

_____

Who do you call first when something bad happens?

_____

_____

What about when something good happens?

_____

_____

When does the verse above say we should talk to God about it?

_____

_____

It's human nature to call on a friend or family member when something big happens. Think about the different people you call for different reasons. I know I call a specific friend when I just want to be right. There are other friends I talk to only when I want to know the truth and am ready to be called out. It's good to talk to our friends and family about what is going on—but it's BEST to talk to God first. When we can allow the Lord to change our hearts, it changes our words and actions, too.

Plus, God is the only one who gets it right every single time. I know there are several situations when I wish I had run to God before calling a friend who ended up giving me bad advice and making the situation even worse.

Even in the toughest situations, run to God! Pray without stopping today, my friend! Keep your heart turned toward God, and it will change the way you respond to people.

PRAYER

Jesus, thank you for being available to talk to all day long. Thank you for loving me and always being here for me. Next time I want to run to someone else first, I ask that you remind me that you are here and you are the only one who loves me perfectly.

"THE LORD LONGS TO BE GRACIOUS TO YOU."

BIBLE JOURNAL

SUPPLY LIST

- sketchbook or piece of paper
- pencils, pens, markers, or whatever you like to draw with

OVERVIEW

Today's project is all about visualizing God as our number one contact!

STEPS

1. Doodle a phone, tablet, or computer in your sketchbook—add as many details as you can!
2. Now, pretend God is a contact. Draw either messages between the two of you or you calling him.
3. Write today's Scripture verse around your drawing.
4. For an extra challenge, take your journal everywhere you go today, and try to write or draw your prayers all day long!

ART NOTES

Drawing Techniques:

Cross-Hatching

Stippling

Lines

Shading

Day 5

Pray then like this: "Our Father in heaven, hallowed be your name. Your kingdom come, your will be done, on earth as it is in heaven. Give us this day our daily bread, and forgive us our debts, as we also have forgiven our debtors. And lead us not into temptation, but deliver us from evil."

Matthew 6:9-13, ESV

Most of us have heard this prayer many times before—and if you're like me, I bet the words roll off your tongue without your really thinking about what you're saying. I believe that we can follow this prayer Christ taught us while still being the unique people God created us to be. Here's a little guide you can use in your Bible journal, drawing from the prayer in the Bible and adding your own unique style!

Calm your heart and listen to God's Word.
Read a Scripture verse and change your spiritual posture.
"Pray then like this: 'Our Father in heaven . . .'"

Raise your hands in worship!
". . . hallowed be your name. Your kingdom come, your will be done, on earth as it is in heaven."

Examine your heart and tell the Lord what you need.
"Give us this day our daily bread . . ."

Ask the Lord for forgiveness and for help forgiving others.
". . . and forgive us our debts, as we also have forgiven our debtors."

Talk to God about what scares or concerns you and ask for protection.
"And lead us not into temptation, but deliver us from evil."

Express what's on your heart!
Draw, paint, or collage your prayers, fears, and praises!

PRAYER
Jesus, thank you for teaching us to pray! I ask, Lord, that you will write these words on my heart and guide my prayer life.

SUPPLY LIST

- canvas, poster board, or large piece of paper
- pencil
- paint or markers
- paintbrush (if using paint)
- cup of water (if using paint)
- black permanent marker

Bubble Letters: These are letters that have space inside the letter—space where we can be creative! The easiest way to start drawing bubble letters is to use a pencil to very lightly write the normal letter you want to draw and then simply outline it with a marker! Remember to go back inside letters that have cut-out parts, like R or A.

OVERVIEW

This weekend we are making signs to remind us daily how to pray!

STEPS

1. With your pencil, sketch out the word *CREATE* in big bubble letters on your canvas.
2. Paint or color the background a cool color (see the Color Family Art Note).
3. Choose warm colors to paint or color inside your letters. Let the paint dry.
4. In black permanent marker, write the description each letter stands for inside each bubble letter. For example, write "Raise your hands in worship!" inside the big bubble *R*.
5. Now put the finished sign somewhere you will use it—maybe by your desk or art area!

ART NOTES

Color Family: Colors belong to the warm family or the cool family. Colors like red, orange, and yellow, that remind us of fire or the sun, are warm. Colors like green, blue, and purple, that remind us of water or the sky, are cool.

Inspired by Our Creator

Nothing in all creation is hidden from God's sight.
Hebrews 4:13, NIV

The more we . . . let (God) take us over,
the more truly ourselves we become.
C. S. Lewis

Day 1

Nothing in all creation is hidden from God's sight.
Hebrews 4:13, NIV

This week we are going to study our heavenly Father's creativity! First things first—let's see what God is saying to us in the very first sentence of the Bible:

In the beginning God created the heavens and the earth.
Genesis 1:1

With your favorite color marker, circle the words **In the beginning**. The word right after this circled phrase is the ONE thing that existed in the beginning. Underline this word—it's God, of course! And now, the verb after God is _____ . Have you ever thought about what this word really means? The very first definition for this word in Dictionary.com is

Create: To cause to come into being, as something unique that would not naturally evolve or that is not made by ordinary processes.

Underline in pink the part of the definition that stands out most to you. "Something unique" stands out to me. Each animal, person, and plant that God has given life to is a unique creation! Just think of all the different

plants and flowers in the world! (There happen to be about 400,000 different types.) Look around you—there are tiny blooms on tall cherry trees and massive petals on magnolia trees. Some plants are hard to grow and are covered in thorns, while others are easy to care for and soft to touch. Each blooms in its own season.

If that is how God clothes the grass of the field, which is here today and tomorrow is thrown into the fire, will he not much more clothe you— you of little faith?
Matthew 6:30, NIV

Write your name in the blank below and then say the phrase out loud!

By his awesome power, God caused something unique to come into being, and her name is

_____ .

PRAYER
Thank you, Jesus, for creating this world and creating ME!

HE KNOWS US FULLY!

BIBLE JOURNAL

SUPPLY LIST

- index card
- watercolor paint or markers
- paintbrush (if using paint)
- cup of water (if using paint)
- black crayon
- pointy stick (like a kabob stick or orange stick) or pen with a retractable tip

OVERVIEW

This week we're going to make a Scripture memory card that reveals hidden colors to remind us that nothing is hidden from God!

STEPS

1. Color one entire side of the index card with watercolors or markers. Let it dry.
2. Cover the colored index card with a thick layer of black crayon.
3. Use a small pointy stick or a pen with the tip pulled in to scratch this week's verse on the card. The stick should scratch off the black to reveal the colors underneath!

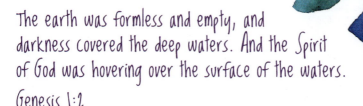

Day 2

The earth was formless and empty, and darkness covered the deep waters. And the Spirit of God was hovering over the surface of the waters.
Genesis 1:2

Are you ever nervous in the dark? I'll be honest, my friends—I often get nervous in the dark! I hear a noise and jump right out of bed! This verse made me start thinking: What exactly is it that makes us nervous about the darkness? Especially since it was an intentional part of our good God's creation!

Let's start to learn how to navigate the dark places in our lives. With a black marker, circle the verb in the verse for today: **hovering**. Dictionary.com says that **hover** means "to wait near at hand." That means . . . in the darkness, God was near at hand.

And we learn later in the Bible (in the very last book of the Bible, in fact), not only was God here first, but he is still here, and he is going before us. Read the verse on the next page and circle the words **is to come**.

"I am the Alpha and the Omega," says the Lord God, "who is, and who was, and who is to come, the Almighty."
Revelation 1:8, NIV

These verses give my heart peace! I love the image of the Lord hovering near me in the dark! And I believe he is waiting near at hand to listen to our prayers.

PRAYER

Jesus, I praise you for creating me and the whole world around me! I praise you for being near to me always and waiting for my prayers. I praise you for going before me and preparing me for what is ahead. I ask that you will remind me that you are close by when I am frightened.

BIBLE JOURNAL

SUPPLY LIST

- dark-colored construction paper or a sketchbook page painted black
- construction paper crayons, oil pastels, or chalk

OVERVIEW

We know God is with us in the dark. He was here before we were even created! Today, we are going to try to illustrate how it feels to trust God even in the dark.

STEPS

1. Imagine your page is the world before God created us—empty and dark.
2. With your crayons, oil pastels, or chalk, draw a large circle that fills the page.
3. Add some squiggly lines to define the continents.
4. Now draw a different pattern inside each continent and ocean. Maybe you could draw plants with different leaf patterns in each continent.
5. With a different color, draw a wavy circle around the earth to represent the Spirit of God.

ART NOTES

Pattern: Anything that repeats itself.

Day 3

God said, "Let there be light," and there was light.
Genesis 1:3

God is writing an exciting and unique story just for YOU. And each of our stories has a beginning, just like in God's creation! Today we read that God created the light. What does light do for us?

_____

_____

_____

_____

_____

_____

You probably wrote that it helps us see! We see color because of light. You probably learned in science class that the light we see is made of a spectrum of colors. Different surfaces reflect different colors of the spectrum. That means . . . before light, the whole world was gray! Everything would have looked so different all of a sudden when the light came on.

Do you remember the first time you saw light? Probably not . . . but what is your earliest memory? Write about it in detail below: Who was there? What were you doing? What did it smell like? What colors do you remember?

_____
_____
_____
_____
_____
_____

Did you know that God planned this specific memory just for YOU? It's the beginning of your story!

PRAYER

Thank you, Jesus, for creating me and my story! Thank you for [insert some of your memories here].

SHINE ON ME, LORD!!

BIBLE JOURNAL

SUPPLY LIST

- sketchbook or piece of paper
- pencil
- black permanent marker
- acrylic paint in the three primary colors: yellow, red, and blue
- paintbrush
- palette to mix colors (can be a disposable plastic plate)
- cup of water

OVERVIEW

Because light creates color, today we are creating a color wheel!

STEPS

1. With your pencil, draw a medium-sized triangle in the center of your sketchbook page or piece of paper.
2. Draw a light circle around the triangle.
3. Draw a small square at each of the three points of the triangle.
4. Along the circle, halfway between each of the three squares, draw smaller triangles.
5. Now, draw a small circle between each small triangle and square along the big circle—you should end up with six of them.

Color Mixing: Mix colors next to one another on the color wheel to create bright new colors. Mix a color with a little of its complement to create more neutral or realistic colors. Mix equal amounts of complementary colors to create browns.

Color Wheel:

6. Trace all the shapes with a permanent marker.

7. Now you're ready to paint! Paint the three small squares with primary colors straight out of the tube—start with yellow, then red, then blue. The primary colors can all be found in nature—and using only these three, we can make all the colors in the world! It's kind of like how all things were created through the Father, Son, and Holy Spirit!

8. Now, mix one primary color with another to make the secondary colors, and paint them in the small triangles between the primaries that make them: yellow + red = orange; red + blue = purple; blue + yellow = green.

9. Last, very carefully on your palette—being sure to leave plenty of each primary and secondary color—mix enough of each primary and secondary color that are connected on the big circle to make the six tertiary colors. For example: mix some yellow with orange to make yellow-orange and paint it in the circle between the yellow square and the orange triangle.

10. If you want to, you can add today's verse to your painting!

ART NOTES

Hue: The "color" we see (for example, yellow, blue, and red).

Color: The way we see light. We often describe a color by its hue, value, or intensity.

Value: The lightness or darkness of the color.

Intensity: The saturation or brightness of the color.

Day 4

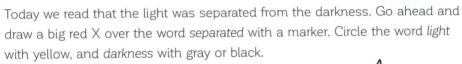

God saw that the light was good. Then he separated the light from the darkness.
Genesis 1:4

Today we read that the light was separated from the darkness. Go ahead and draw a big red X over the word *separated* with a marker. Circle the word *light* with yellow, and *darkness* with gray or black.

Dictionary.com defines *separate* this way:

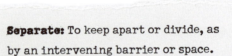

Separate: To keep apart or divide, as by an intervening barrier or space.

So, the verse is saying that God took the beautiful, colorful light and created a _____ to divide it from the darkness. He built a wall down the middle! He created the darkness, but

gave it strict boundaries and rules to follow. What are some rules for darkness we can see every day?

_____

_____

_____

_____

_____

_____

Did you know that in some places in the world it's dark or light more than others? When it's winter in Alaska, there are days when the sun never comes up, and in summer, there are days when it never sets! The boundaries for light and dark are different all over the world!

I like the rules right where I am! Just about half-and-half light and dark. I love to be outside on a sunny day, and I love to rest when night falls. God's good plan helps us to work and rest too.

PRAYER

Thank you, Jesus, for creating the light and the dark! I praise you for planning time for me to rest and time to work! Please help me trust you today!

HE IS BIG ENOUGH.

BIBLE JOURNAL

SUPPLY LIST

- sketchbook or piece of paper
- red crayon
- black crayon
- paint, markers, colored pencils, crayons, or anything else you want to color with
- paintbrush (if using paint)
- cup of water (if using paint)

OVERVIEW

We are going to do a project that expresses our need for both the night and the day!

STEPS

1. Draw a line straight down the middle of your page with a red crayon.
2. Label one side of the paper "Day" and the other side "Night."
3. With a black crayon, draw one continuous, wiggly line that goes all over the page, overlapping itself as much as you like!
4. On the "Night" side, use only cool colors like blue, purple, green, black, and gray to color in each shape that you made with your wiggly line.
5. On the "Day" side, color in each shape with warm colors like red, orange, yellow, brown, and tan! (See the Color Family Art Note on page 42.)
6. Think about how God makes both day and night beautiful in their own way.

Day 5

God called the light "day" and the darkness "night." And evening passed and morning came, marking the first day. . . . Then God said, "Let the waters beneath the sky flow together into one place, so dry ground may appear." And that is what happened. God called the dry ground "land" and the waters "seas." And God saw that it was good.

Genesis 1:5, 9-10

GOOD. It was GOOD. We are going to talk a lot about TRUTH in this study—and without truth, nothing can be truly good. Before the Fall (when Adam and Eve disobeyed God and sin entered the world) everything was good. Open your Bible and scan the rest of Genesis 1. How many times does it say "and God saw that it was good?"_____

A bunch! Everything God created was good—even people. Look up verse 31 and fill in the blank:

God looked over all he had made, and he saw that it was _____ good!

Everything was good until he got to us, and then we were very good. It makes me smile a little just thinking about it! I feel that way sometimes while I paint, don't you? I paint and paint, adding a little of this and a little of that, and then all of a sudden it feels right—it feels "very good."

PRAYER

Jesus, I praise you for all of creation. I praise you for creating it all good. Thank you for creating this world full of colors and patterns that inspire us to create. Jesus, please continue to inspire me to create and to worship you!

BIBLE JOURNAL
weekend challenge

- canvas, or poster board or large piece of paper fixed to a drawing board with masking tape around the edges
- paintbrushes in various sizes (I would recommend ¼ inch up to 1½ inch, but any size will do!)
- paint
- palette to mix colors (can be a disposable plastic plate)
- cup of water
- paper towels

OVERVIEW

This weekend your challenge is to get out in God's creation for inspiration! If you can't go outside, find a landscape picture that inspires you to paint! A painting of an outside scene is called a landscape, and if you paint outside, it's called en *plein air*—a fancy French term the Impressionists (like Monet!) used.

STEPS

1. Paint a horizontal line two-thirds of the way down the page with a light color like yellow, using the smallest brush you have. This is your horizon line—where the sky meets the ground. This line and the others you sketch will be painted over, so relax and have fun during this part—no pressure!

2. Continue using your light-colored paint to block in big things you see, starting at the bottom of your page (or foreground). Draw in trees, houses, hills, bushes, fences, etc. Don't get into any detail—just use basic shapes.

3. The objects that are at the bottom of your canvas are closest to you and should be the biggest. When you are finished with this layer, begin painting in what is behind them (your midground). Objects in each layer behind the foreground should get smaller and smaller.

4. Now add the objects that are far away and closest to the horizon line. These should be smaller and higher than similar objects in the foreground.

5. Stand back from your canvas and look at your shapes. If there are too many on one side, you may want to add more to the other to create balance in your composition.

6. Begin mixing the colors you see (use your color wheel!) and paint the colors where you see them!

7. If you don't like a color, don't give up—just wipe it off or wait for it to dry and paint over it.

8. Last, go back and add small details with your smallest brush. Add brushstrokes for leaves, flowers, and even blades of grass in the foreground.

9. For extra credit, try layering colors and adding highlights that create value in each shape (see the Value Art Note on page 16).

ART NOTES

Perspective: How an artist creates the illusion of a 3-D space in a 2-D work of art. Perspective techniques include overlapping objects, making objects smaller as they get closer to the horizon line, and adding atmospheric effects (making "faraway" objects less detailed and closer in color to the sky).

Horizon Line: The imaginary line where the sky meets the land.

Vanishing Point: Located on the horizon line, this is the point where all the imaginary lines in a picture plane meet. It can create a focal point.

Background: Things "farthest" from the viewer in a work of art. These things will be the least saturated, highest on the picture plane, smallest in relative size, and overlapped by parts of both the foreground and midground.

Midground: Things between the foreground and the background in a work of art. They will be overlapped by the foreground but overlap the background. They will be less saturated than the foreground but more saturated than the background. They will be higher up on the picture plane than the foreground, but lower than the background.

Foreground: What is "closest" to the viewer in a work of art. It will be larger, brighter, more saturated, and closer to the bottom of the picture plane—it could even go off the picture plane.

Created to Feel

We do not have a high priest who is unable to empathize with our weakness, but we have one who has been tempted in every way, just as we are—yet he did not sin.

Hebrews 4:15, NIV

The great thing to remember is that though our feelings come and go, (God's) love does not.

C. S. Lewis

Day 1

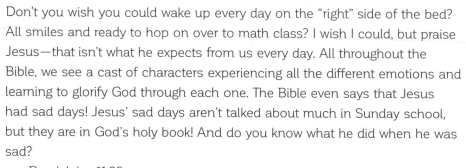

> We do not have a high priest who is unable to empathize with our weaknesses, but we have one who has been tempted in every way, just as we are—yet he did not sin.
> Hebrews 4:15, NIV

Don't you wish you could wake up every day on the "right" side of the bed? All smiles and ready to hop on over to math class? I wish I could, but praise Jesus—that isn't what he expects from us every day. All throughout the Bible, we see a cast of characters experiencing all the different emotions and learning to glorify God through each one. The Bible even says that Jesus had sad days! Jesus' sad days aren't talked about much in Sunday school, but they are in God's holy book! And do you know what he did when he was sad?

　　Read John 11:35:

Jesus _____.

_____

_____

_____

_____

_____

Now go back to the beginning of John 11 and read verses 1-3. Why was Jesus sad?

I love this story because it really helps me relate to Jesus! I've never walked on water, but I have cried because I was sad, just like he did. But he also had days that were so great that words like *fabulous*, *epic*, and *mind-blowing* don't even begin to describe them! Turn to Matthew 3 and read verses 16-17. Here's the cool part . . . drumroll, please: "He saw the Spirit of God descending like a dove and alighting on him. And a voice from heaven said, 'This is my Son, whom I love; with him I am well pleased'" (NIV). I don't think Jesus was crying that day (well, maybe tears of joy)! I would love to hear my parents say these words to me, and even more so my heavenly Father! I would be bursting with PURE JOY, and I am sure Jesus was as well.

PRAYER

God, thank you for loving me. I praise you for sending a Savior who can sympathize with my weakness and struggles. I pray that you will teach me how to glorify you both when I am happy and when I am sad.

HE COLLECTS ALL OUR TEARS.

BIBLE JOURNAL

SUPPLY LIST

· index card
· pen
· fine-point markers
· ink pad or marker

OVERVIEW

This week you're going to use your own thumb-print to decorate your Scripture memory card, as a reminder that you were uniquely created by a God who understands and cares for you.

STEPS

1. Write this week's verse on your index card with a pen or fine-point marker.
2. Press your thumb into an ink pad, or color it with a marker. Use your thumbprint to create different shapes on the index card—birds, butterflies, flowers, hearts, or whatever you want!
3. When the ink has dried, use fine-point markers to add details to your thumbprint creations.

Created to Feel

Day 2

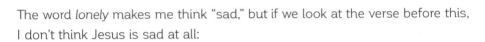

Jesus often withdrew to
lonely places and prayed.
Luke 5:16, NIV

The word *lonely* makes me think "sad," but if we look at the verse before this, I don't think Jesus is sad at all:

The news about him spread all the more, so that crowds of people came
to hear him and to be healed of their sicknesses.
Luke 5:15, NIV

So Jesus became known for all the great things he was doing, and then he withdrew to lonely places? Why do you think he would do that?

_____

_____

_____

_____

Jesus had lots of work to do while he was on earth, and he had to get it all done in only three years! He had come into the world to save the lost, bring the truth, and redeem God's people! That's a lot of pressure. I feel pressure just working on special paintings! Will the person who asked me to create it for them even like it? I can't imagine the pressure of being the Savior of the world!

In just three years, Christ changed the planet forever—and I bet it felt overwhelming sometimes. Jesus was 30 at the time he started his ministry, and according to Google a 30-year-old person needs 7 to 8 hours of sleep each night. But younger people need even more than that: 9 to 11 hours of sleep a day for most school-age kids. That's more than a third of your day!

God has raised us up for great purposes, but we still need balance, reflection, and REST! Next time you get stressed or tired, remember that even the Savior of the world needed some alone time to pray and recharge!

PRAYER

Jesus, thank you for creating me for your high purposes! I praise you for giving me the perfect example of dealing with stress! Please help me set aside time to rest and pray, just as Christ did during his time on earth!

TAKE TIME TO
- REST &
- RESPOND

BIBLE JOURNAL

SUPPLY LIST

- music (Ask an adult to help you find an example of slow music and an example of fast music. I love the Christian album *Without Words: Synesthesia* because I can really focus on the pace and rhythm of each song.)
- sketchbook or piece of paper
- pencil
- permanent marker
- eraser
- paint, markers, colored pencils, crayons, or anything else you want to color with
- paintbrush (if using paint)
- cup of water (if using paint)

OVERVIEW

Today we are going to look at the contrast between fast and slow—and how we can find balance between the two!

STEPS

1. Find a fast song and a slow song. Listen to each all the way through.
2. Listen to the fast song again and use your pencil to draw lines on your sketchbook page that illustrate the movement you hear.
3. Do the exact same thing with the slow song.
4. If you need some ideas, ask an adult to help you research Wassily Kandinksy. I love how his art comes to life in this video: https://youtu.be /aMiiKLyIR88.
5. Go back and trace over your favorite fast and slow lines with permanent marker and erase the rest.
6. Use your other materials to color in the new shapes and spaces you have created.

Day 3

I tell you not to worry about everyday life—whether you have enough food to eat or enough clothes to wear. For life is more than food, and your body more than clothing. Look at the ravens. They don't plant or harvest or store food in barns, for God feeds them. And you are far more valuable to him than any birds!

Luke 12:22–24

Can you even imagine a bird flying around fully dressed in clothes?! Just picture it for a second . . . maybe it's a redbird with a flannel button-down, skinny jeans, and Chuck Taylors! LOL! And why aren't there bird drive-through restaurants on the corner of every magnolia tree?

Today's verse is saying that these birds fly and sing and build nests all day and don't worry about food or clothing . . . because God gives them what they need each day. He sends a worm at just the right time, and he has already dressed the birds in clothes way nicer and more beautiful than the flannel shirt and skinny jeans I have on!

On the next page, fill in the first blank with the thing you worry about most and the second blank with your name:

Jesus, help me not to worry about

_____

today. Your Word tells me that I can
trust you. Since I can see how you take
care of even tiny birds, I trust that
you will take care of me. I am delighted
that your Word says that

_____

is of value to you!

PRAYER

Pray the prayer to the left with your name in it out loud! (Close the door if you're scared your little brother will make fun of you.) If there is something you truly need, pray that God would bless you with it, and prayer-fully ask your friends or family. When God provides, remember to PRAISE HIM!

BIBLE JOURNAL

SUPPLY LIST

- scratch paper
- pencil or pen
- magazines, pictures, and photos (anything to collage with)
- scissors
- sketchbook or piece of paper
- glue
- permanent marker

OVERVIEW

We are going to create a PRAISE collage today to help us remember all we have to be grateful for!

STEPS

1. PRAY and ask God to remind you of all the people, places, and things he has blessed you with. Make a list.
2. Find images of these people, places, and things (or images that remind you of them).
3. Cut out your images and create a composition with them. Maybe all your people are sitting on the front porch that you love!
4. Carefully glue each image to your sketchbook page or piece of paper.
5. Use a permanent marker to write the title "PRAISE COLLAGE" and/or write out our verse for today at the top of your paper.

Collage: An artistic composition made of various materials (such as paper, cloth, or wood) glued on a surface.

Day 4

Shout for joy to the LORD, all the earth.
Worship the LORD with gladness; come before
him with joyful songs.
Psalm 100:1-2, NIV

Hey there! I'm having one of those days where I can just feel in my soul that God is GOOD. Have you ever had a day like that? The sun is shining, the flowers are blooming, birds are singing . . .

God gives us lots of different days, and when we have a GOOD day, we should give it back to God! We should do just what the psalm above says (fill in the blanks below):

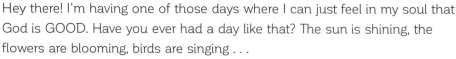

_____ for joy to the LORD, all the

earth. _____ the LORD with gladness;

_____ before him with joyful

_____ .

I was blessed to live in West Africa for a short season. There was a phrase people would say there to greet one another. One person would walk by and say, "God is good!" and the other would reply, "All the time." I think they are saying this to remind each other that God is good when we don't feel it just as much as when we do.

So what am I going to do on this GOOD day? I'm going to turn on my praise music (if you're not sure what to listen to, I am lovin' me some *Red Sea Road* by Ellie Holcomb right now) and paint my praise! I'm going to sing and worship and come before the Lord with joyful song and painting! Will you join me?

PRAYER
God, you are good, ALL the time! Help me to give the joyful days back to you in praise, and help me to remember you are good even when *I* don't feel it.

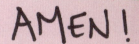

AMEN!

BIBLE JOURNAL

SUPPLY LIST

- your favorite praise and worship music
- sketchbook or piece of paper
- spray bottle with water
- watercolor paint or markers
- paintbrush (if using paint)
- cup of water (if using paint)
- salt
- pen or fine-point marker

OVERVIEW

Today we are painting colors that represent PRAISE!

STEPS

1. Get your praise music going!
2. Pray and invite God into your space.
3. Use your spray bottle to wet the page so every inch is damp.
4. Choose colors that represent praise to you (a lot of people think that yellow is the "happiest" color) and drop or dot them on the wet page.
5. Watch the colors spread on the page—imagine that is our praise!
6. Keep adding colors and playing.
7. Add a dash of salt in a few places and let it dry.
8. After your paper dries, dust the salt off into a trash can to see the fun texture left behind.
9. Last, write out our verse from today somewhere on the page in your best writing or calligraphy!

Calligraphy: A decorative handwriting or hand-lettering technique. To make your own calligraphy, try to give your up- and downstrokes different line weights. Most calligraphy is much thinner on the upstrokes and gradually thicker on the downstrokes.

ART NOTES

Color Theory: The practical science of color mixing and the effects of color choices. See the other color art notes on pages 42, 56-57, and 211 for specific examples.

Day 5

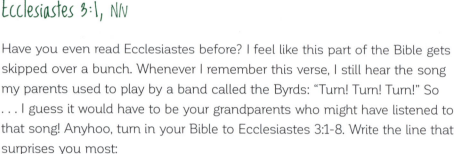

There is a time for everything, and a season for every activity under the heavens. Ecclesiastes 3:1, NIV

Have you even read Ecclesiastes before? I feel like this part of the Bible gets skipped over a bunch. Whenever I remember this verse, I still hear the song my parents used to play by a band called the Byrds: "Turn! Turn! Turn!" So . . . I guess it would have to be your grandparents who might have listened to that song! Anyhoo, turn in your Bible to Ecclesiastes 3:1-8. Write the line that surprises you most:

_____

_____

_____

_____

When I was your age, mine would have been "a time to weep and a time to laugh; a time to mourn and a time to dance." I really believed that I was supposed to act happy all the time. If I was weeping, I thought something was wrong. But God's Word says there is a time for everything . . . even "a time for war and a time for peace."

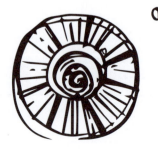

The truth is, God's Word is full of people feeling all sorts of emotions. Our emotions are real and important—but NOT more important than God's Word. Even though I may *feel* like eating every single chocolate chip cookie on the cookie sheet, it's probably not the healthiest choice I could make. Let's see what God's Word says about trusting our emotions: "The heart is deceitful above all things, and desperately sick; who can understand it?" (Jeremiah 17:9, ESV).

When we are making difficult choices, we can use our emotions to navigate, but we will need a guide to make sure our hearts aren't deceiving us! What can we use to keep our emotions in check? (Hint: Sunday-school answer here!)

_____

The word of God is alive and powerful. It is sharper than the sharpest two-edged sword, cutting between soul and spirit, between joint and marrow. It exposes our innermost thoughts and desires.

Hebrews 4:12

PRAYER
God of all creation, help me to listen to my emotions and let them guide me to times of rest or action. But, Lord, remind me of your Word and help me use it to keep my heart accountable.

WE caN NOT CHANGE OUR OWN ♡'s

BIBLE JOURNAL
weekend challenge

OVERVIEW

This weekend we are continuing to reflect on our emotions by creating a self-portrait!

STEPS

1. Take a picture of yourself making an expressive face—exhausted, overjoyed, crazy, or anything else you are feelin', sister!
2. Print the picture out and cut the top of your head wide open like a cartoon—your head is opened up for everything to come out!
3. Glue the picture down on the left side of a spread in your sketchbook or the left side of a piece of paper.
4. With your pencil, draw a horizontal line going right across the middle of your paper.
5. Draw a vertical line through your photo going straight down between your eyes.
6. Redraw this grid on the right side of the page or spread and then work, box by box, to redraw the picture of yourself using your pencil (see the Facial Proportions Art Note on page 215).
7. Start light—you can always add darker values, but it's harder to get lighter. Erase any stray lines.
8. When you are finished drawing, write one of the verses from today spiraling or spilling out of your open head.
9. Think about what the Scripture in your mind would say about the emotion on your face.

SUPPLY LIST

- phone or digital camera
- printer and printer paper
- scissors
- glue
- pencil
- eraser
- sketchbook or piece of paper

Portrait: A painting or drawing of a person.

Self-Portrait: A likeness of oneself, usually focusing on the face.

Created to Think

When I consider your heavens, the work of your fingers, the moon and the stars, which you have set in place, what is mankind that you are mindful of them, human beings that you care for them?

Psalm 8:3-4, NIV

Aim at Heaven and you will get earth "thrown in": aim at earth and you will get neither.

C. S. Lewis

Day 1

> When I consider your heavens, the work of your fingers, the moon and the stars, which you have set in place, what is mankind that you are mindful of them, human beings that you care for them?
> Psalm 8:3-4, NIV

Have you ever been outside at night, away from city lights, and looked up to see all the stars? I grew up in rural Alabama, where we can easily get away from man-made light. I love looking up at the stars in awe, thinking about how BIG our world is and how excited I am just to be a part of it. Looking into the stars gives me the same feeling as looking out on the sea or staring into a wide green pasture. It somehow gives me peace, knowing that I am just a small part of something much bigger!

Look again at our passage for this week. The psalmist is writing about this very thing! Circle the words **mindful** and **care for them** and then let's unpack those parts. According to Dictionary.com, being mindful of something means you are attentive, aware, or careful. What are some things in your life you are mindful of or care for? (Maybe siblings, pets, or a ministry you are involved with?)

_____

_____

_____

_____

_____

The first thing that comes to my mind is my plants—if I forget to water my orchids and hydrangeas, they will wilt. I have to think of them often and do for them what they can't do for themselves. The Bible tells us that we are always on God's mind. We're going to spend the rest of this week learning what Scripture says about *our* minds!

Now, I want you to rewrite the verse in your own words. Here's my paraphrase as an example:

> When I consider the wide open fields and all the beautiful sunsets you have created, I can't believe that I am even a thought in your mind, God!

Now you try!

_____

_____

_____

_____

_____

PRAYER
Jesus, thank you for being mindful of me. Help me to realize that I was created with a purpose and am loved deeply by you, my Creator!

BIBLE JOURNAL

SUPPLY LIST

- book on astronomy or phone or computer with Internet access
- waxed paper
- ruler
- scissors
- acrylic paint
- paintbrush
- cup of water
- toothpick
- permanent marker
- index card, cardboard, or card stock (optional)
- tape or glue (optional)

OVERVIEW

We're going to write this week's verse on a mini galaxy painting to remind us that the God who made the moon and stars cares about us.

STEPS

1. Look at photos of galaxies in a book or online. Notice how the colors swirl together and how brighter stars stand out.
2. Cut a piece of waxed paper 3 inches wide and 5 inches long.
3. Paint a beautiful galaxy on the waxed paper. You can use some black, but make sure to use lighter colors as well (so your verse will show up later). Use a toothpick to add dots of white paint for stars. Let the picture dry.
4. Turn your painting over and write this week's verse on the other side with a permanent marker (make sure to write over lighter-colored paint so the words show up).
5. If you want, tape or glue your painting to an index card or piece of cardboard to make it sturdier.

Day 2

He who searches our hearts knows the mind of the Spirit.

Romans 8:27, NIV

Now, we know that we are created in the image of God. If God says his Spirit has a mind, and that's important enough to mention in the Bible, our minds must be pretty important too. Have you ever thought about why God gave you a mind? He gave us eyes to see, a heart to feel, and a mind to think, invent, write, and create with! But the most important thing we can do with our minds is choose to be mindful of Christ and glorify him.

Those who are dominated by the sinful nature think about sinful things, but those who are controlled by the Holy Spirit think about things that please the Spirit.

Romans 8:5

From this verse we can see that there are two kinds of things our minds can think about. In the verse above, circle the two kinds of things and then fill in the chart below:

If we are controlled by the	we think about
sinful nature	
Holy Spirit	

Look up Galatians 5:19-21 and make a list of actions of the sinful nature:

_____

_____

_____

_____

Now read Galatians 5:22-23 and make a list of the fruit of the Spirit:

_____

_____

_____

_____

Compare the two lists. Are they similar or different?

The sinful nature wants to do evil, which is just the opposite of what the Spirit wants. And the Spirit gives us desires that are the opposite of what the sinful nature desires. These two forces are constantly fighting each other, so you are not free to carry out your good intentions.
Galatians 5:17

God created us with unique and powerful minds that are capable of amazing things. But the choice is ours to use them for his glory or our own.

SUPPLY LIST

- any type of colored or painted paper
- pencil
- scissors
- glue
- sketchbook or piece of paper
- construction paper crayons or paint pens

BIBLE JOURNAL

OVERVIEW

Our project today is simply creating an illustration of all that we read in the devotional!

STEPS

1. With your pencil, draw the silhouette (a flat shape like a shadow) of a brain on your colored or painted paper.
2. Cut the brain shape out around the outside. Before you start, fold your paper in one small place near the pencil line so you can start the cut and not have to cut into the background.
3. Take BOTH the silhouette of the brain AND the piece of paper it was cut from and glue them down in your sketchbook or on your piece of paper next to each other. The background shape is the negative space, and the brain silhouette is the positive space.
4. On the positive piece write out the fruit of the Spirit in bright colors using crayons or paint pens.
5. On the negative piece write out some of the things on your list of desires of the sinful nature in dull colors.
6. Consider the POWER of what we put in our brains and how it can change our perspective and lead to changing our actions.

Space: The general areas or shapes in a work of art.
Positive Space: The areas created by the main objects in a work.

Negative Space: The areas surrounding the main objects in a work; the background.

ART NOTES

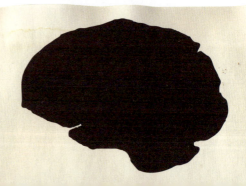

Day 3

Letting your sinful nature control your mind leads to death. But letting the Spirit control your mind leads to life and peace.
Romans 8:6

Yesterday, we unpacked how the tension between our sin nature and the Holy Spirit can shape our thoughts. Today we are digging into where each thought process leads us and how we can live in the Spirit!

Looking deeper into what our minds were created for makes it easy to say, "Yes! I want life and peace!" But when we're in the middle of a situation, the choice doesn't feel so easy. When we get injured, broken, embarrassed, or shamed, even over little things, it's easy to spiral into a mind-set that isn't glorifying to the Lord. Sometimes when someone else seems to have more friends than I do, I'm jealous! Then, something (my sin nature) starts helping me come up with reasons I deserve to have more friends than she does.

When we feel angry or sad, we may start to feel sorry for ourselves and think, *I didn't deserve that!* Our minds can quickly spiral out of control when we listen to our sin nature. We need to daily (sometimes hourly!) check our minds to see who or what is guiding our thoughts. But how do we live according to the Spirit even when all these negative thoughts come into our minds? Let's read Paul's encouragement to the Roman Christians (and us!).

(Circle the words **live** and **die** in this passage as you read.)

Therefore, dear brothers and sisters, you have no obligation to do what your sinful nature urges you to do. For if you live by its dictates, you will die. But if through the power of the Spirit you put to death the deeds of your sinful nature, you will live. For all who are led by the Spirit of God are children of God.

Romans 8:12-14

PRAYER
Jesus, I surrender my mind to you, to truth, to your Spirit! I ask now that you would teach me your ways and truths, and that you would help me be mindful of my thoughts.

The path of resisting our sin nature leads to _____. And the path of listening to our sin nature leads to _____.

So let's live by the Spirit! The Bible says in John 4:24 that if we live by the Spirit, we will worship in _____ and in _____.

So now let's pray for wisdom and learn the TRUTH, so we can live in the Spirit!

BIBLE JOURNAL

SUPPLY LIST

- sketchbook or piece of paper
- pencil
- marker

OVERVIEW

We are going to draw two spirals today, one going in and one going out, to illustrate the way this world impacts our hearts.

STEPS

1. With your pencil, draw two spirals that fill two pages next to each other. On the first page, start on the left side and spiral clockwise in toward the center. On the other page, start in the center and spiral clockwise out, ending on the right side.
2. On the spiral on the left, write the negative thoughts that make you sad and make you want to hide (or you can draw pictures of them if you want).
3. On the spiral on the right, start by writing the word **truth**, and then write a Scripture verse from the devotions in this book.
4. Trace your lines and words with a marker. Play with the weight of the lines—for example, the lines could be thicker on one side to make it appear closer to you.
5. Pray for the Spirit to show you when your sinful nature is bringing your thoughts down, and pray for God's truth to always help rescue you!

Created to Think

Day 4

Walk by the Spirit, and you will not gratify the desires of the flesh.

Galatians 5:16, NIV

After all that we've learned so far this week, why in the world does this verse say "walk"? Why don't we RUN or PUSH or MAKE HAPPEN by the Spirit? If we are going to win the battle for our minds, don't we need to get a head start or pack a bag for the event?

This reminds me of one of my favorite stories from the Old Testament. Let's flip to Exodus 16 and read verses 4-30. Fill in these blanks:

Each day the people can go out and pick up as much food as they need for _____. (verse 4)

The people gathered the food morning by morning, each _____.

And as the sun became hot, the flakes they had not picked up melted and disappeared. (verse 21)

The Israelites called the food _____. (verse 31)

102

GROSS ☒☒

So what's the point? God gave the Israelites what they needed *when* they needed it. When they tried to work ahead and store away more manna than they needed for one day, "it [became] full of maggots and had a terrible smell" (verse 20). Eeewww!!!

Also notice that the manna came first thing in the morning! God provided enough manna for each person to gather what they needed for just that day—no more, no less. Talk about daily bread! And guess what? God still meets us in the same way—in the newness of the morning he prepares a feast for us, full of truth and love in just the right amount for *today*.

PRAYER

God, thank you for your provision of daily bread, spiritual and physical. I pray that you will grow a hunger in me to walk with you daily and seek your will above my own.

BIBLE JOURNAL

SUPPLY LIST

- sketchbook or piece of paper
- scissors
- pencil
- permanent marker
- colored pencils

OVERVIEW

Someone said to me recently, "God hasn't lost his recipe for manna!" I love that—he is still so faithful to provide for us each day just what we need. Today, I want you to make some "manna recipe cards" to share with friends.

STEPS

1. Cut a piece of paper into quarters and ask God who needs an extra dose of his truth today.
2. Use a pencil to write one of your favorite Scripture verses on each piece in your personal hand lettering (see the Lettering and Calligraphy Art Notes on pages 20 and 83 if you need a reminder). Once the letters look the way you want them to, trace over them with a permanent marker.
3. Write a small note about what to do with the verse—maybe read it three times before school?
4. Use your colored pencils to draw a little illustration of the verse. For example, if you write Galatians 5:22-23, you may choose to draw a bowl of fruit.
5. Give the cards to your friends to encourage them!

Day 5

The peace of God, which transcends all understanding, will guard your hearts and your minds in Christ Jesus.

Philippians 4:7, NIV

God's peace can guard our hearts! But why would the peace of God "transcend understanding"? Let's look at a few more Scriptures:

Look up Romans 16:20 and write who the God of peace will crush:

_____

_____

_____

_____

Look up John 14:27 and write what does NOT give peace like God does:

_____

_____

_____

_____

(Side note: the verses above talk about two of the believer's three enemies. Do you remember our third enemy? Look up Jeremiah 17:9. Yep, it's our own hearts! Have you ever realized how powerful you are? You are so powerful and important that you have three enemies. Good thing your Friend is way more powerful than any of them!)

Look up 2 Peter 1:2 and write how we can have grace and peace:

_____

_____

_____

_____

If you smush it all together, you will get something like:

> God's peace will crush _____, it
> is not of _____ , and an abundance
> of it comes through the _____
> of God and of Jesus our Lord.

So we can receive peace through knowing God and Jesus our Lord! It is something beyond this world, something the Holy Spirit gives, and according to John 3:34, "God gives the Spirit without limit" (NIV).

All we have to do is ask God for his peace that comes through the truth in his Word. When we seek him, he is faithful to guard our minds! Praise God!

GOD WILL GUARD OUR MINDS!

BIBLE JOURNAL
weekend challenge

SUPPLY LIST

- sketchbook or piece of paper
- pencil
- canvas, poster board, or large piece of paper
- acrylic paint
- paintbrush
- cup of water

OVERVIEW

Today, I want us to think about how God gives his Spirit "without limit," so we are going to play with proportion! Proportion in art is the size relationship between two or more objects. Incorrect proportion may include an apple as big as a house or a bug larger than people. (Sometimes it's fun to make proportions incorrect on purpose!) God's Spirit is so much greater in proportion to anything we could imagine!

STEPS

1. Review the art notes on pages 65 and 211. Now think of the largest building you know of and sketch it in your sketchbook or on a piece of paper.
2. Paint the same building at the bottom of your canvas as small as you can.
3. Add the horizon line behind it and maybe some teeny tiny trees around it to fill up the bottom edge of the canvas.
4. Now, we are going to paint the sky! The best way to paint clouds is by layering paint colors. In real life clouds are transparent—think of fog on the ground. To get the effect of light shining on real clouds, we are going to start with a background sky color and add layers on top.
5. The background layer is the darkest—go outside and look at the sky! Pick a blue and add some white to lighten it and add a little orange to neutralize it. (Adding a complementary color

makes our colors look more like real life—the sky isn't really ever the exact color that comes out of a tube!) Now paint the whole canvas increasingly dark as you go up.

6. Take an hour break or let your painting dry overnight.

7. Mix some cloud colors: white with a little blue for the middles, white with a little yellow and maybe even the tiniest amount of pink for the highlights on each cloud, and white with a little gray and blue for the bottom shadows.

8. Start by painting small clouds close to the bottom of your sky. Remember to look at real clouds for inspiration—each cloud is unique!

9. Near the top of the painting, let the clouds fade into night sky with stars.

10. Look at how BIG the sky is compared to your building! Take in how BIG our God and the peace he has to offer are. Praise him for that!

Landscape: An outside scene.

ART NOTE

Worshiping Our Creator

You are worthy, O Lord our God, to receive glory and honor and power. For you created all things, and they exist because you created what you pleased.

Revelation 4:11

You cannot love a fellow-creature fully till you love God.

C. S. Lewis

Day 1

You are worthy, O Lord our God, to receive glory and honor and power. For you created all things, and they exist because you created what you pleased.
Revelation 4:11

So we know we were created for a higher purpose—to serve and bring glory to God—but what's a girl to do in the meantime? Let's look back at *how* God created us to get some clues:

God said, "Let us make human beings in our image, to be like us. They will reign over the fish in the sea, the birds in the sky, the livestock, all the wild animals on the earth, and the small animals that scurry along the ground." So God created human beings in his own image. In the image of God he created them; male and female he created them.
Genesis 1:26-27

If we were created in God's own image, wouldn't he look like us? In his books *The Great Divorce* and *The Lion, the Witch and the Wardrobe*, my absolute favorite author C. S. Lewis compares God to a waterfall and a

lion. I guess I look more like a lion than a waterfall, since we both have a pulse and two eyes and all. But, wow—a waterfall feels just like God: big and powerful, continually washing us clean, clear, and pure.

Even if we can't know what God looks like, we know we were made in his image because we were created for relationships. Circle the word us in the verse above. Have you picked up on that before? There was an "us" before humans were even created. We know from John 1:1 that the Word (Jesus) was around before Creation. Some Bible scholars believe the "us" here refers to the Trinity—God the Father, God the Son, and God the Holy Spirit—while others think he's talking to his heavenly court of angels. I'm not going to pretend to have been there, but I can say from Scripture I am certain God the Father was not alone; there was fellowship and relationships before Creation. Since we are created in God's image, we are created for relationships too. We were created for relationships with other people, but most of all with God himself!

BIBLE JOURNAL

SUPPLY LIST

- piece of paper
- ruler
- scissors
- crayons (ones you can take the wrappers off)
- leaves (look for different shapes and sizes)
- permanent marker
- index card, cardboard, or card stock (optional)
- tape or glue (optional)

OVERVIEW

Today we're going to write our verse over textures we find in nature to remind us of all the things God created.

STEPS

1. Cut your paper down to index-card size (3 inches by 5 inches).
2. Take the paper wrappers off your crayons.
3. Choose a leaf and put it under your paper. Holding your crayon horizontally, make a rubbing of the leaf.
4. Repeat with different leaves and colors. Think about how each leaf is unique and wonderfully made.
5. Write this week's verse over your rubbings with a permanent marker.
6. If you want, tape or glue your rubbing to an index card or piece of cardboard to make it sturdier.

Day 2

Worship the LORD with gladness;
come before him with joyful songs.
Psalm 100:2, NIV

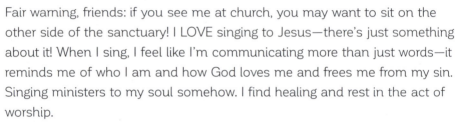

Fair warning, friends: if you see me at church, you may want to sit on the other side of the sanctuary! I LOVE singing to Jesus—there's just something about it! When I sing, I feel like I'm communicating more than just words—it reminds me of who I am and how God loves me and frees me from my sin. Singing ministers to my soul somehow. I find healing and rest in the act of worship.

But sadly, I cannot match a pitch to save my life! I just "make a joyful noise unto the LORD" (Psalm 100:1, KJV).

Another creative way we can worship God is found in Genesis 2:15. God put man in the garden to "_____ it." What do we do when we work and take care of a garden? We plan, dig, plant, and water, whether it's flowers, veggies, or fruit! God wants us to CREATE things and beautify his world! And there are so many ways to beautify the earth—we can make beautiful food; plant or arrange flowers . . . even the way we

dress ourselves can be an art! In Song of Songs, we read how our female bodies were beautifully created! The way we decorate our rooms, the candles we burn, even the smile we wear can beautify a space. In ALL things, let us worship our heavenly Father!

Let everything that breathes sing praises to the LORD!
Psalm 150:6

Are you breathing right now? I thought so!

PRAYER
I praise you, Father, for you are King of kings and Lord of lords! You are Alpha and Omega, beginning and end. You, my God, are God, and I am not.

BIBLE JOURNAL

SUPPLY LIST

· objects for your still life

· canvas, poster board, or large piece of paper

· paint (any type)

· paintbrush

· cup of water

OVERVIEW

We are going to beautify and create! During the Protestant Reformation in the sixteenth century, the newly reformed churches didn't want to create paintings or stained glass that had Jesus or Mary or any characters from the Bible because they felt that it was too close to making an idol. Instead, they painted still lifes that communicated truths the Lord put on their hearts. Today, we are going to set up our own still lifes to paint.

ART NOTES

Still Life: A drawing or painting of arranged objects.

STEPS

1. Look around your house or yard for things that represent your faith. (If your adults in charge are okay with it, maybe you could even go to the store to get some fresh flowers or fruit.)

2. Set up your still life: consider color scheme and variety of texture. Overlap some objects to create interest. (Research works by Dutch still life painter Pieter Claesz for more ideas.)

3. Step back from your still life and imagine how it will fit inside the rectangle of your canvas. You want it to fill the area, but not get too crowded.

4. With yellow paint (so you can paint over it), sketch your tabletop and then your objects, starting with what is closest to you. Objects closer to the back will be covered or overlapped by some other objects.

5. Mix paint to make the colors you see and fill in your page (see the Value Art Note on page 16 for more on creating highlights and shadows and the Color Mixing Art Note on page 56 for more on creating new colors).

Variety: The use of several different elements to create interest in a composition.

Balance: The distribution of visual weight across a composition.

Focal Point: The part of the composition that catches the viewer's attention first; it will often stand out by contrasting with the background.

Contrast: Placing opposite or very different visual elements together in a way that creates visual interest and leads the viewer's eyes to what the artist wants to emphasize (for example, black next to white, complementary colors next to one another, hard and smooth surfaces together).

Day 3

You must worship no other gods, for the LORD, whose very name is Jealous, is a God who is jealous about his relationship with you.
Exodus 34:14

Because our hearts are created to worship, we can't turn it off if we try! If we stop worshiping God, our hearts will start searching for something else to worship. You've probably heard this word before: *idolatry*, or idol worship.

In the Old Testament, we see God's people, the Israelites, build an idol right after God faithfully led them out of Egypt AND PARTED THE RED SEA for them! I feel like I would remember to worship God after something like that. Moses leaves for a minute to grab the Ten Commandments (kind of a big deal), and the Israelites turn right around and start creating their own idol: a golden calf (see Exodus 32). And later in the Old Testament, we read about three friends named Shadrach, Meshach, and Abednego who decide NOT to worship an idol—and it results in their being thrown in a blazing furnace (see Daniel 3). Today, we don't see many people bowing down to golden idols in town squares or bringing sacrifices to statues of animals . . . so have we stopped committing idolatry?

Not hardly. An idol can be anything you spend too much time, money, attention, or energy on. For some people it's popularity. If you just can't miss a party or spend all your time thinking about who likes you and who doesn't, this may be your idol. Maybe it's a sport you are involved in—do you

think about it when you're hanging out with family or friends, do tons of extra practice, daydream often about trophies or medals you are hoping for? Maybe your idol is you! Maybe you spend so much time fixing your hair or picking out clothes that you're always late out the door. An idol can be *anything* that you value more than God, even just in that moment. Take a minute to pray about what your idols are. Do not be ashamed—write them down and talk to the Lord about them. He won't shame you or reject you—he loves you and wants to help you!

If you think you are standing strong, be careful not to fall. The temptations in your life are no different from what others experience. And God is faithful. He will not allow the temptation to be more than you can stand. When you are tempted, he will show you a way out so that you can endure. So, my dear friends, flee from the worship of idols.
1 Corinthians 10:12-14

PRAYER
Jesus, I praise you for creating me to worship! I am so sorry for all the other things and people I choose to worship instead of you. Please forgive me and help me put YOU back in the center of my heart.

HE WONT
SHAME
YOU!!!

BIBLE JOURNAL

SUPPLY LIST

- magazines, newspapers, printed images to collage
- computer with Internet access (optional)
- printer with printer paper (optional)
- sketchbook or piece of paper
- pencil
- scissors
- glue
- markers or colored pencils

OVERVIEW

Today we are going to reflect on some of the things we have made into idols by creating an idol collage.

STEPS

1. Grab some magazines or print pictures off of the computer of all the things that you sometimes make into idols.
2. Draw a horizontal line on your paper about halfway up.
3. Below the line, collage all the things you think or worry about too much—let them overlap, mix, and mash up!
4. Above the line draw a chair, but not just any chair—a throne! You can look up pictures to use as models or just use your imagination. Either way, use markers or colored pencils to make it fancy, with lots of details and colors.
5. Then draw either a cross or how you picture Jesus on the throne (see Revelation 4 for a description of Christ on his throne). Ask Jesus to come back to the throne of your heart!

Day 4

A time is coming and has now come when the true worshipers will worship the Father in the Spirit and in truth, for they are the kind of worshipers the Father seeks.

John 4:23, NIV

Did you know that there was a time when people were allowed to worship God only in certain places? The verse above is taken from a very profound story in the Bible. Open up your Bible to John 4:7-26 to read the background.

Who are the two people that meet at the well?_____ and

_____

Who did Jesus ask the woman to get? _____

So then a funny thing happens—Jesus knows her story before she tells him! She realizes he is special, and thinks he may be a prophet, so she asks him the real answer to where she should worship. (The Samaritans had been arguing with the Jews about this question for years. The Samaritans

worshiped God on a certain mountain, and the Jews had their Temple.) We hear all sorts of opinions around our dinner tables, at school, and at church. This woman was doing the very thing we should do: asking God for herself! She asked Jesus to give her the truth, not realizing that the Truth was standing right in front of her!

Jesus simply told her, "Believe me, dear woman, the time is coming when it will no longer matter whether you worship the Father on this mountain or in Jerusalem" (verse 21). Jesus was talking about what would happen through his death on the cross: freedom to come directly to God!

When Christ died, the curtain in the Temple was torn—bringing down the barrier between us and God. When Jesus died, he freed us to worship him anywhere in the Spirit and in truth! Praise him!

PRAYER
Lord, thank you for creating me to worship. Thank you for sending your Son to die so that I can worship you anywhere and everywhere!

WOW

BIBLE JOURNAL

OVERVIEW

Today we are going to praise Jesus wherever we are!

STEPS

1. Grab your sketchbook or paper, a fine-point marker, some watercolor pencils, and a watercolor pen and take them with you for the day!
2. Find moments throughout the day to praise Jesus in the Spirit and truth by both reading Scripture and writing your praises out in marker.
3. Start drawing the things you are praising God for—maybe a beautiful day or sweet friends at school!
4. Using your watercolor pencils or paint, begin with the lightest values and work to the darks (see the Value Art Note on page 16).
5. If you are using watercolor pencils, mix the colors with your watercolor brush pen or water and brush!

SUPPLY LIST

- sketchbook or piece of paper
- fine-point marker
- watercolor pencils or watercolor paint
- watercolor brush pen or paintbrush and jar of water

Day 5

Jesus led [the disciples] to Bethany, and lifting his hands to heaven, he blessed them. While he was blessing them, he left them and was taken up to heaven. So they worshiped him and then returned to Jerusalem filled with great joy. And they spent all of their time in the Temple, praising God.

Luke 24:50-53

Sometimes it's hard to worship—like when we're frustrated, tired, or busy. Sometimes it's just not easy to worship a God who could change the situation that is making me sad but doesn't seem to be doing anything about it. When that happens, it feels impossible for me to bring my heart to a place of worship. I have to ask God for help! The verse today is one example of how Christ's disciples handled a similar situation. It's after the Cross, when Christ was taken up to heaven. He appeared to many of his followers on several different occasions, spoke with them, and blessed them, and then he left.

The Savior the Jews had spent centuries praying for had come and gone. He LEFT, and then what did they do? _____

You got it—they *worshiped* him. I would have been tempted to sit around feeling sad and wondering why Christ had to leave.

We can apply two lessons from this situation to our lives: (1) Jesus had given them the Holy Spirit—part of him would always be able to minister to them. (2) The disciples could worship Jesus because they TRUSTED him. They trusted that he was sovereign and good, even though they may not have understood their current situation.

It's the same for us—even when we don't feel like worshiping, we can remind ourselves that God is sovereign and good. We can trust that even if we can't see why or how right now, he is at work in whatever is making us frustrated, tired, bitter, or busy. And we have the Holy Spirit to call on!

PRAYER

Holy Spirit, thank you for reminding me to worship in the Spirit and in truth even when I don't feel like it. I praise you, Father, Son, and Holy Spirit, for your goodness!

ASK GOD FOR HELP.

BIBLE JOURNAL
weekend challenge

SUPPLY LIST

- canvas, poster board, or large piece of paper
- paintbrushes in several sizes
- modeling paste or toilet paper, water, and glue
- paint
- paper towels

OVERVIEW

This weekend we are going to work with layers of texture on canvas to help us see how God is shaping us in different ways and as a reminder to call on him no matter how we feel.

STEPS

1. Grab all your materials and find a place that doesn't mind a mess.
2. PRAY! Ask God what he is teaching you right now—what do you need to praise him for?
3. Take the modeling paste (or your toilet paper dipped in watered-down glue) and spread it on the canvas. Use your largest brush to make texture marks on the paste or paper.

Movement: The path created by colors, textures, or brushstrokes to lead the viewer's eye through a work of art.

4. Build up the texture. Think of the movement of your brushstrokes—horizontal lines appear more stable, while diagonal or zigzag lines have more dynamic energy (see the Movement and Texture Art Notes for more info).
5. Repeat this step with increasingly smaller brushes, leaving some of each mark made by each brush.
6. Let the modeling paste or toilet paper dry—this may take a whole day.
7. When it's dry, think of the white textured canvas as our hearts that God is shaping. Start adding layers of watercolor or watered-down paint to your textured canvas.
8. Use paper towels to wipe some paint away and add more texture.
9. Use a dry-brush technique to add some more texture to your canvas. This just means making sure your brush is all the way dry and there is no water in the paint—it gives you a very wispy brushstroke with wild, unpredictable ends.
10. Continue to add layers, while letting part of each layer show through to the end.

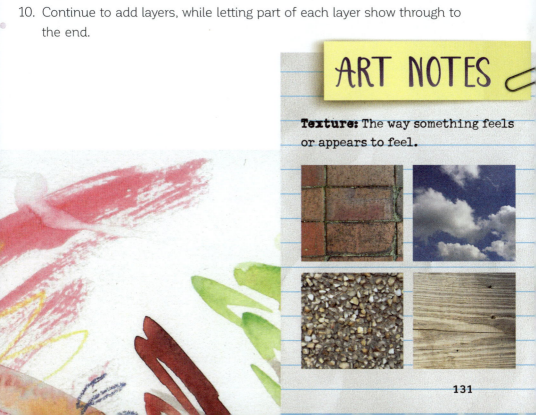

ART NOTES

Texture: The way something feels or appears to feel.

Creating Space for God

God so loved the world that he gave his one and only Son, that whoever believes in him shall not perish but have eternal life.
John 3:16, NIV

Imagine yourself as a living house. God comes in to rebuild that house. At first, perhaps, you can understand what He is doing. He is getting the drains right and stopping the leaks in the roof and so on; you knew that those jobs needed doing and so you are not surprised. But presently He starts knocking the house about in a way that hurts abominably and does not seem to make sense. What on earth is He up to? The explanation is that He is building quite a different house from the one you thought of—throwing out a new wing here, putting on an extra floor there, running up towers, making courtyards. You thought you were going to be made into a decent little cottage: but He is building a palace. He intends to come and live in it Himself.

C. S. Lewis

Day 1

God so loved the world that he gave his one and only Son, that whoever believes in him shall not perish but have eternal life.

John 3:16, NIV

Well, hello, my friend! Do you hear that? "Look! I stand at the door and knock. If you hear my voice and open the door, I will come in, and we will share a meal together as friends" (Revelation 3:20). Your almighty Creator is knocking! Did you know that God is always standing at your door? It's true! No matter what you may have done to hide from him, no matter what you have inside that you think might scare him away, he will always be standing at the door to your heart knocking, waiting . . .

Can you even imagine waiting at someone's front door as long as the God of the universe has been waiting at yours?! I am not even patient enough to knock twice sometimes! "Quit your lollygaggin'!" my dad always says . . . but not our heavenly Father. He is patiently waiting for YOU to open the door. Not demanding, not banging—just whispering and knocking. He has already done all the work through Christ on the cross.

He has reconciled you to himself through the death of Christ in his physical body. As a result, he has brought you into his own presence, and you are holy and blameless as you stand before him without a single fault.

Colossians 1:22

All you have to do is answer. So, what do you think? Are you ready to make space for God in your heart? Want to let him in? Pray the prayer on the right or one in your own words.

If you have prayed this prayer before, now is a good time to talk to God about what parts of your life you need to recommit to him!

If you asked Jesus into your heart today for the first time, share with a friend, your family, or a church leader! Ask them to tell you their stories of salvation. Ask them to help you take your next steps of faith with Jesus.

PRAYER

Jesus, I want to make space for you and invite you into my heart. Thank you for waiting for me and loving me, even when I have been unlovely. I confess that I cannot be good on my own, and I am in desperate need of a Savior. I know that your death on the cross is the only way I can have a relationship with you. I ask you to forgive all the sin in my life and send your Holy Spirit to live in my heart.

BIBLE JOURNAL

SUPPLY LIST

- two pieces of construction paper in complementary colors (like yellow and purple—see the Color Scheme Art Note on page 211.)
- ruler
- scissors
- pencil
- tape or glue
- fine-point markers
- index card, cardboard, or card stock (optional)

OVERVIEW

Today we're going to write our memory verse inside a door to remind ourselves that Jesus is knocking on the door of our hearts, asking us to create space for him.

STEPS

1. Cut the two pieces of construction paper to index-card size (3 inches by 5 inches).
2. Use your pencil and ruler to draw a door and door frame on the darker piece of construction paper.
3. Cut the door away from the door frame on three sides so it can fold back and open like a door.
4. Tape or glue the door frame to the lighter piece of construction paper (make sure not to put any glue on the door!).
5. When the glue is dry, write this week's verse inside the door in marker.
6. Use your markers to add details and decorations to your door and door frame!
7. If you want, tape or glue your creation to an index card or piece of cardboard to make it sturdier.

Day 2

Have mercy on me, O God, because of your unfailing love. Because of your great compassion, blot out the stain of my sins. Wash me clean from my guilt. Purify me from my sin.
Psalm 51:1-2

This week is all about creating space for God in our hearts. Yesterday we invited him in, so now let's make sure we have cleaned out a good spot for him!

The verse above is a prayer asking God to help us "blot out the stain of [our] sins" or clean out the mess in our hearts. The next sentences ask him to wash us _____ from our guilt and _____ us. When Christ claims his throne in our hearts, he's going to do some laundry, dust the curtains, and sweep under the couch!

Since the moment humans first disobeyed God, sin has been part of our world. Everything God intended for good can now somehow be used for evil. Think of music, for example: music was created by God to worship him! But there are so many song lyrics in the world today that have very little to do with praising God. Take a moment to pray the verse above and ask God

what he wants you to clean out of your heart or life. Maybe it's some anger you are holding on to or a bad habit that doesn't glorify God. Take your time, quiet your heart, and listen.

If we confess our sins to him, he is faithful and just to forgive us our sins and to cleanse us from all wickedness.

1 John 1:9

PRAYER

Father God, thank you for sending your one and only Son to die on the cross to pay the penalty for the sin in my heart. I pray that you would fill my heart with healing, faith in your Son, and eternal life.

BIBLE JOURNAL

SUPPLY LIST

- image of a heart
- sketchbook or piece of paper (or a piece of blue construction paper)
- blue marker or pen (or white chalk or crayon)

OVERVIEW

Today you are going to draw some blueprints for the home in your heart!

STEPS

1. Find a picture of an actual heart and draw the outline of the shape with a blue marker or pen (or trace the shape on your paper).
2. Divide your heart into "rooms" for all the different parts of your life—school, family, sports, ballet, etc.—but leave a room empty right in the center, with a doorway to each of the other rooms.
3. Draw a symbol for each part of your life in its room. For example, you could draw a pencil or a book for school, a soccer ball for sports, and a little house for family.
4. Make the room in the center your prayer room— where Jesus lives in your heart. Draw a throne or crown in there to show that Jesus reigns in your life. Then draw a cross in all the other rooms to show that Jesus goes with you and is Lord of every part.

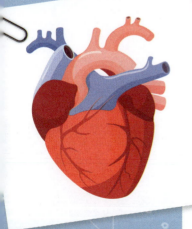

Day 3

Create in me a clean heart, O God.
Renew a loyal spirit within me.

Psalm 51:10

CREATE is the theme for this whole book (obviously), but what does it really mean in this verse—and what is going to happen to our hearts?

So I went back to good ol' Dictionary.com:

> **Create:** To cause to come into being, as something unique that would not naturally evolve or that is not made by ordinary processes; to cause to happen; arrange, as by intention or design.

Underline any words in this definition that stand out to you. (Mine were *unique*, *processes*, *intention*, and *design*.) Next, circle all the verbs.

Do you see what I see if we enter these words into the verse?

> (Cause to come into being as something unique, not by natural processes, arranged with intention and design) in me a clean heart.

See it? It's saying that we need a supernatural process to clean our hearts. It's saying we need JESUS to change our hearts! We cannot clean our own hearts or just try to be good enough. Christ has already done all the work for us to be cleansed and redeemed!

God so loved the world that he gave his one and only Son, that whoever believes in him shall not perish but have eternal life.

John 3:16, NIV

Every day we desperately need reminders that it is Christ alone who is willing and able to change our hearts! Praise him because his work is DONE!

PRAYER

Thank you, Jesus, for doing all the dirty work for me. Help me to remember that the work is done, and all I have left to do is trust YOU!

BIBLE JOURNAL

SUPPLY LIST

- scratch paper
- pencil
- sketchbook or piece of paper
- white glue
- paintbrush
- watercolor paint
- cup of water

OVERVIEW

Today we are going to make an illustration that reminds us that God has an intentional design for our lives, even when we can't see it!

STEPS

1. Instead of using glue to stick things together, today we are going to draw with it!
2. First, practice making patterns with a pencil on a piece of scratch paper so you know your design will look nice (see the Pattern Art Note on page 53).
3. Draw a grid that fills a whole page of scratch paper.
4. Fill in each grid box with a pattern!
5. Now draw your grid box and patterns with glue in your sketchbook.
6. Let the glue dry.
7. Go back and paint with watercolor in between all your glue lines.
8. Think of the glue as God's intentional design for your life—consider how it's all connected, planned, and uniquely YOU!

Day 4

I am the true vine, and my Father is the gardener.
John 15:1, NIV

I love the picture this verse paints in my mind! Us sharing life with Christ as a branch on his vine, with God the Father watching over us. Our lives connected with those of our loved ones—all through God's creation and redemption.

But then we come to the next verse: "He cuts off every branch in me that bears no fruit, while every branch that does bear fruit he prunes so that it will be even more fruitful" (John 15:2, NIV).

Wait, what?! Can we just white out this verse and pretend it's not in the Good Book? I want to go back to that pretty picture, with everyone together in harmony. I've always been told if something hurts, drop it! If I touch the cookie sheet right out of the oven with my bare hands—ouch! I may drop the pan right then and there! But we can't do that with Scripture, as much as we may want to. And this verse says one of the ways we will know we are connected to the true Vine is that God the Father will prune or even cut us off. But . . . I thought God was LOVE!

I learned at flower-arranging class a while back that gardeners and florists are taught to cut off all leaves and branches that aren't producing fruit

or flowers. These stems and leaves take nutrients from the fruit the gardener is trying to grow or from the blooms the florist wants to last until the big event this weekend! God's love is higher than any other we will experience. He prunes parts of our lives to feed the things that are producing fruit! God is lovingly encouraging us to grow in places and ways that produce the BEST fruit—fruit that brings glory to him!

When you produce much fruit, you are my true disciples. This brings great glory to my Father.
John 15:8

PRAYER

Jesus, thank you for being the true Vine! Thank you for giving me life and energy, and thank you for loving me enough to prune the parts of my life that aren't bringing you glory. Please help me remember you are the good gardener next time I hurt. Help me trust your plan!

BIBLE JOURNAL

SUPPLY LIST

· leaf or fruit on a branch or picture of one

· sketchbook or piece of paper

· colored pencils

OVERVIEW

Today we are going to draw a leaf or fruit and think about how the vine or branch it was connected to gave it shape!

STEPS

1. Go outside to find a leaf or fruit on a branch (or find a picture of one).
2. With your yellow colored pencil (so you can color over lines if you mess up or change your mind) draw the outline of the branch. Consider drawing it at a diagonal across the page to create a more dynamic movement (see the Composition Art Note on page 9 and the Movement Art Note on page 130).
3. Then, take the time to look for all the colors in the leaves, fruit, and branch—I bet there are more than you thought!
4. Overlap and blend with your pencils to create new colors!
5. While you color in the leaf or fruit, think about how the branch gives life to the leaves and how if the branch wasn't "true," the leaves would wither.

Day 5

Jesus responded, "You say I am a king. Actually, I was born and came into the world to testify to the truth. All who love the truth recognize that what I say is true."
John 18:37

The word *truth* gets thrown around all the time. I want us to make space in our hearts for the real truth . . . but how do we know what that is? How can we know that we have the whole story? Before we can even begin to discuss, much less answer, any big questions, we have to start with the basics: where can we find the TRUTH?

In our verse today, Jesus himself says he came to testify to the

_____. How does he know the truth? Where did he hear it? And . . . where did it come from? Turn in your Bible to John 1 and fill in these blanks:

• In the beginning was the _____, and the _____ was with God, and the _____ was God.

John 1:1, NIV

The _____ became flesh and made his dwelling among us.

John 1:14, NIV

For the law was given through Moses; grace and _____ came through _____ _____. No one has ever seen God, but the one and only Son, who is himself God and is in closest relationship with the Father, has made him known.

John 1:17-18, NIV

This verse makes for some important math: The Word = God = Truth = Jesus Christ.

The truth can be found in God's Word, the Holy Bible. Wow. You've got one of those right in front of you! Now that you have invited Jesus into your heart and cleared space for him, it's time to start letting his truth soak in.

And we can rely on his truth when asking questions and making big decisions in life.

My child, never forget the things I have taught you. Store my commands in your heart. If you do this, you will live many years, and your life will be satisfying.

Proverbs 3:1-2

PRAYER

Father God, I need your truth, love, and grace in my life. Will you see me as you see your Son, who lived and died so I could be with you? God, will you walk with me every step of today?

AMEN!

BIBLE JOURNAL
weekend challenge

OVERVIEW

We are going to paint as if we are "walking" with Jesus—one step at a time.

STEPS

1. Start by painting the whole canvas one dark color, like teal or magenta, in thick brushstrokes.
2. While the paint is still wet, take a pencil or stick and carve this week's Scripture verse into the paint.
3. Wait for this layer to dry, but don't get attached—we have a lot more steps to follow!
4. Use gesso or white paint and paint over three-fourths of the painting. Yup—paint over half of it, all together or in several different areas.
5. Next, take out your watercolors and paint on top of the gesso. Choose colors that remind you of something you are frustrated about.

6. When that's dry, paint over half of your canvas with gesso or white paint.
7. When it's almost dry, use bubble wrap or a stick to add random marks all over.
8. Then paint out one-fourth of the canvas with gesso or white paint.
9. When the paint is dry, use a black marker or paint to draw the outline of the tree in your picture with one continuous contour line (without picking up your marker). Start your line on the left side of the canvas, wrap up into the shape of a tree, adding a few details along the way, and then exit off the right side of the canvas.
10. Step back and look at your painting. Add more if you like.
11. Think of the tree and the layers of paint as TRUTH that is stored deep in your heart and growing each day.

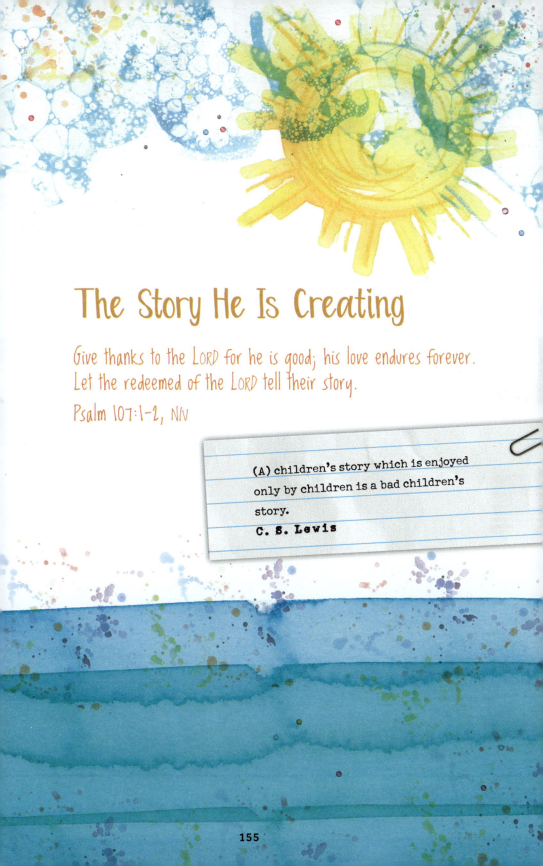

The Story He Is Creating

Give thanks to the LORD for he is good; his love endures forever. Let the redeemed of the LORD tell their story.

Psalm 107:1-2, NIV

(A) children's story which is enjoyed only by children is a bad children's story.

C. S. Lewis

Day 1

*Give thanks to the LORD for he is good;
his love endures forever. Let the redeemed
of the LORD tell their story.*
Psalm 107:1-2, NIV

This week is all about stories—stories from the Bible and how they can help us tell the story God is writing for us! All the stories we read in the whole Bible—even the Old Testament—point us to Jesus and show the BIG and UNIQUE story God is writing just for you and me! So where do we start? At the beginning. The first five books of the Bible (Genesis, Exodus, Leviticus, Numbers, and Deuteronomy) are called the books of the Law or the Pentateuch.

Let's start our stories like God starts his: in the book of Genesis! In Genesis we read that God created the world and saw that it was GOOD. He had given Adam and Eve everything they needed to live happily ever after in the Garden of Eden.

Think about your story. Do you remember a time in your life when everything seemed good?

As a little girl, I remember singing "Silent Night" by candlelight with my family on Christmas Eve. I could look left or right and see everyone smiling

SHARE YOUR STORY: you never know who or how it will — encourage others!

(except that time my sister's candle caught her hair on fire!).

Now, what is one memory of a time you realized everything wasn't okay? I'll never forget the first time I heard my parents argue. I felt in my soul that something was wrong.

Did you know that *both* of these experiences were part of God's plan? There are moments of "creation" and "fall" in our own lives. After God finished his good creation, Eve decided to eat the forbidden fruit, and all our lives changed forever. Our hearts were created to walk and talk with God, just like Adam and Eve did. But when they disobeyed God, it created a separation between God and people, and allowed sin, pain, and death into our lives.

But do not fret, my friend! This action set into motion God's plan for a Savior—one who would come centuries after the fruit had been eaten, one who could and would redeem what was lost—even you and me.

PRAYER

God, I praise you for giving us your Word so that we can read and understand who you are. God, I am so sad that our world is fallen and full of sin, but I praise you for setting into motion a plan for redemption!

BIBLE JOURNAL

SUPPLY LIST

- index card
- pen or fine-point marker
- paint, markers, colored pencils, crayons, or anything else you want to color with
- paintbrush (if using paint)
- cup of water (if using paint)
- stickers, ribbons, sequins, or whatever you want to decorate with
- glue

OVERVIEW

Today you're going to create a memory-verse bookmark! Whenever you read a story this week, you'll be reminded that God is writing his story in the world and in your life.

STEPS

1. Turn your index card so it's vertical.
2. Write this week's verse on the card with a pen or fine-point marker. You can highlight key words by using a different color or decorating them if you like.
3. Use the supplies you've collected to decorate your verse bookmark! (Just make sure to use materials that won't rub off and mark the book you put it in.)

Day 2

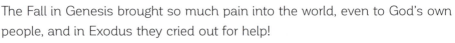

I am the LORD your God, who rescued you from the land of Egypt, the place of your slavery.

Exodus 20:2

The Fall in Genesis brought so much pain into the world, even to God's own people, and in Exodus they cried out for help!

In the first chapters of Exodus, the Israelites (also called Hebrews) were slaves in Egypt. So God sent a baby . . . but not Jesus yet. It was Moses. He was born to an Israelite family, but at the worst time ever. Pharaoh had ordered that all Israelite baby boys be killed! But God saved Moses. You may know this part: when Moses was born, his mother hid him for three months and then set him afloat in a basket on the Nile River, not far from Pharaoh's palace, right where Pharaoh's daughter would be outside bathing and find sweet baby Moses. What a picture of God's grace in the middle of such suffering! Moses was adopted as a son of the princess and raised in the palace—and his own mother got to care for him when he was a baby! Then things took a turn:

Many years later, when Moses had grown up, he went out to visit his own people, the Hebrews, and he saw how hard they were forced to work. During his visit, he saw an Egyptian beating one of his fellow Hebrews. After looking in all directions to make sure no one was watching, Moses killed the Egyptian and hid the body in the sand.

Exodus 2:11-12

Moses messed up. He probably struggled to know where he belonged: he called the Hebrews "his own people," but he was raised by Egyptians! Major identity crisis! When it all blew up in his face, he did what I would do: he RAN! He basically hid until the Lord revealed himself in the burning bush. Moses didn't want to at first, but he ended up believing God, returning to Egypt, and freeing his people (who happened to be God's people too!). You might know the rest of the story: Moses led the Israelites out of Egypt, through the Red Sea, into the wilderness, and right up to the edge of the Promised Land!

Think about your story. Can you think of a time you ran from God or struggled to believe him? How did God reveal himself to you?

PRAYER

I praise you, Father, for working all things together for your glory! I am in awe of how you can use every part of my story to bring about your will! I praise you for giving us your Word so that we can read about all you have done for us!

BIBLE JOURNAL

SUPPLY LIST

- scratch paper
- scissors
- tape
- sketchbook or piece of paper
- paint
- paintbrush
- cup of water
- objects that will make a cool texture, such as plastic forks and knives, cardboard, sticks, or leaves. (Just make sure to ask your adult for permission to paint with them!)

OVERVIEW

Today we are going to make a piece that represents the struggles we face and how God works in the midst of them.

STEPS

1. Cut the shape of a cross out of your piece of scratch paper and tape it to the center of a page inside your sketchbook or on a piece of paper. (Put tape along every edge of the cross so it's completely sealed down.)
2. Paint different colors onto your texture examples and stamp them around and on your cross. Use colors that make you think of struggles you face or that the Israelites faced in the Bible.
3. Fill the whole page with stamps of different textures and colors.
4. When your paint is dry, peel up the cross to reveal a reminder of God working in the middle of the suffering and confusion.

Day 3

It is a burnt offering, a food offering, an aroma pleasing to the LORD.

Leviticus 1:9, NIV

After the Israelites fled from Egypt, they needed help remembering God's covenant and how to make atonement for their sin (how to "make it up" to God): through sacrifice. God taught the Israelites all the steps it takes to be in relationship with him . . . step by step by gruesome, bloody step.

It's hard for me to think about the word *sacrifice*. I don't usually kill even the meat I eat at home. I go to the grocery store and choose food that already looks like food. I'll never forget the time I was in West Africa, teaching children in a village about Jesus, when one little boy was called away by his mom only to return with blood splattered across his chest! I was shocked!! But he was smiling ear to ear, like nothing at all had happened. When I asked him about it, he calmly said he had just killed a chicken for dinner. WHAT?!?! This little boy was maybe five years old and killing animals and then going to Bible school with blood on his clothes!

Somehow, this event reminded me of sacrifice in the Old Testament. It was difficult and messy and had to be pretty smelly, too. Throughout the book of Leviticus, Moses goes through all the details for different types of sacrifices. Some were burnt, some chopped, some set out different ways. (And I think giving up chocolate for a day is a sacrifice!)

But, as the Bible says, sacrifice is needed to pay for sin. "It is the blood, given in exchange for a life, that makes purification possible" (Leviticus 17:11). So why don't we sacrifice an animal when we sin anymore? Because all our sin debt was paid in full by Jesus' death on the cross: the ultimate sacrifice! "God's will was for us to be made holy by the sacrifice of the body of Jesus Christ, once for all time" (Hebrews 10:10). I don't know about you, but I am beyond grateful that we don't have to sacrifice animals anymore!

I asked Jesus into my heart when I was sixteen. I soon discovered that there were several things I had to give up or take on to keep my eyes on Christ. I had to give up some activities, some friends, and a good bit of my pride. I knew that God was calling me to completely give up worrying about what other people thought. But the biggest sacrifice of all? God called me to start getting up early and spending time with him, *before* school.

Think about your story. What are some things you had to change when you gave your life to Christ? Or what is the Lord calling you to sacrifice now?

HE KNOWS US FULLY!

PRAYER

God, thank you for sending Jesus as the sacrifice for my sins! Thank you, Lord, that we don't have to sacrifice animals anymore! Please show me what needs to change in my life to live in relationship with you. Thank you, Lord, for writing this story of redemption!

BIBLE JOURNAL

SUPPLY LIST

- sketchbook or piece of paper
- markers
- pencil, pen, or whatever you like to write with

OVERVIEW

Today we are going to think about sacrifice as part of our relationship with God. What is one thing that you LOVE (TV, video games, shopping, ice cream?) that you are willing to sacrifice today?

STEPS

1. With your markers, draw a picture of the thing you are sacrificing/giving up just for today.
2. Every time you want to watch/use/eat/play with this thing, instead open to the page with its picture and write a short prayer praising God!
3. At the end of the day, your page should be full of prayers!
4. Think about how sacrifice can be a GOOD thing, after all—and praise God for making the ultimate sacrifice for us.

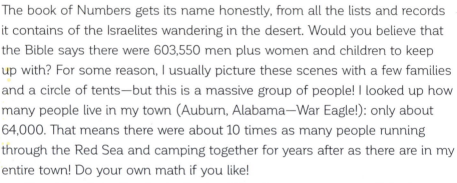

Day 4

Your children will be like shepherds, wandering in the wilderness for forty years.

Numbers 14:33

The book of Numbers gets its name honestly, from all the lists and records it contains of the Israelites wandering in the desert. Would you believe that the Bible says there were 603,550 men plus women and children to keep up with? For some reason, I usually picture these scenes with a few families and a circle of tents—but this is a massive group of people! I looked up how many people live in my town (Auburn, Alabama—War Eagle!): only about 64,000. That means there were about 10 times as many people running through the Red Sea and camping together for years after as there are in my entire town! Do your own math if you like!

So while all the lists in the book of Numbers may seem, well, boring, they must be pretty important if God called Moses and Aaron to keep them! All the people were divided into family groups. Each family group was important. The Levites, for example, were chosen to serve God as priests. They were to care for the Tabernacle and move it reverently from stop to stop along the journey.

All of the families in Israel played a role in history. But only one would contain the ancestors of Jesus. If you flip to Matthew 1, you can see a list of the ancestors of Jesus. It includes some pretty interesting folks—prostitutes, slaves, murderers, etc. But that lineage backs all the way up to the book of Numbers. Maybe this is why God had Moses and Aaron keep tabs on everyone?

So, what's all this wandering got to do with us? Just like the Israelites, we sometimes forget our journey is to the Promised Land—heaven. We lose sight of the goal, and we fall away from the faith. How do we learn to "wander" or walk well through days and years of following Christ? By keeping our eyes on Christ one step at a time. Walk with me?

Think about your story. How are you wandering with Christ? What is your walk with him like today?

PRAYER

God, thank you for creating me special, unique, and with purpose! Thank you for all the men and women who are part of your plan for my life. I pray, Lord, that you would continue to help me be grateful for ALL of my family. I pray for those members who do not know you—I pray that you would speak to their hearts! Help me to love them the way you do.

BIBLE JOURNAL

SUPPLY LIST

- sketchbook or piece of paper
- pencil
- permanent marker
- watercolor paint
- paintbrush
- cup of water

OVERVIEW

Jesus was a descendant of a man named Judah—the tribe of Judah often mentioned in the Bible was named after him. Each piece of Jesus' ancestry is an important part of God's plan. And the same goes for YOU! Today, you are going to make a family tree!

STEPS

1. Find a relative (or several of them) and ask them to help you with your family tree—they can sit with you while you sketch!
2. Open your sketchbook or grab a piece of paper and write your name at the top with a pencil.
3. Write your siblings' names next to your name.
4. Below that, write your parents' names and draw lines from your name and your siblings' names to their names.
5. Add your parents' siblings next to them.
6. Add their parents' names below and draw connecting lines.
7. Write your grandparents' siblings' names next to theirs and their parents' names below and draw connecting lines.
8. Repeat this through all generations you know of. Whenever you get to a place where you can't remember (Was your great-aunt named Bernice or Bernadette? Or, as in my case, Cherry Belle or Eunice?), ask your parents or another relative. They may already have some documents you can copy notes from!
9. When you have all the information, turn to a new page or piece of paper and start drawing your tree with the permanent marker. Begin at the

trunk with the oldest relatives you can come up with. (For example, if you know the names of all eight of your great-grandparents, list all four couples on the trunk, making sure to put your mom's grandparents and your dad's grandparents next to each other.)

10. Write the names of their kids on big branches, and the names of *their* kids on branches coming out from those branches, and so on, until you get to you!

11. When you are done, paint with watercolors over each branch and name.

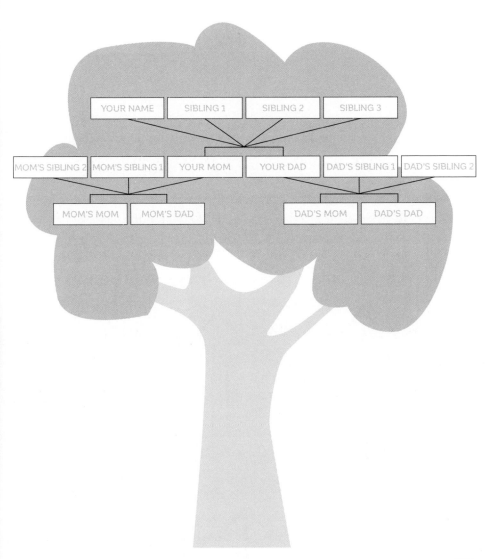

Day 5

> Today I have given you the choice between life and death, between blessings and curses. Now I call on heaven and earth to witness the choice you make. Oh, that you would choose life, so that you and your descendants might live! You can make this choice by loving the LORD your God, obeying him, and committing yourself firmly to him.
>
> Deuteronomy 30:19-20

FINALLY! the Israelites were probably thinking. *We made it! To the land flowing with milk and honey . . . the Promised Land!* And you, my sweet sister, have made it to the end of our survey of the Pentateuch, the books of the Law! Hopefully, you've also started putting together the precious story of creation, fall, redemption, and hope that God is writing just for YOU.

So what is God saying in the verse above? He gave the Israelites the choice between _____ and _____, between _____ and _____ .

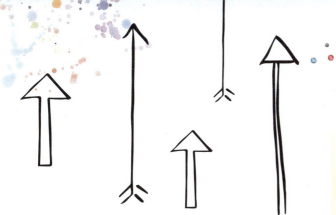

He's telling them that this isn't the easy road! Just as they followed God in the wilderness, so they will need to follow him in the Promised Land! Then he gives the biggest reminder that they and we need to hear EVERY DAY:

Oh, that you would

_____ _____ .

Deuteronomy 30:19

But there's good news in Deuteronomy too: "The LORD your God will raise up for you a prophet like me from among your fellow Israelites" (18:15). This future prophet was not just any prophet! Who do you think this book is pointing us to once again? Jesus!

Think about your story. How are you relying on Christ today? What is he teaching you now? What can you share to encourage others?

PRAYER
Lord, thank you for your Word and all the truth and hope you give us through it. I pray, Lord, that you would continue to remind me of your goodness and grace every day.

BIBLE JOURNAL
weekend challenge

SUPPLY LIST

- sketchbook or piece of paper
- pencil, pen, or whatever you like to write with
- markers or colored pencils

OVERVIEW

Today you're going to write your own story!

STEPS

1. Start by filling in the chart on the next page with notes.
2. Take your notes and write them out in sentences in your sketchbook.
3. Keep your story somewhere safe. This is your testimony of God's work in your life, and you never know when you will want to share it!
4. You can also illustrate your story with markers or colored pencils if you like!

Book:	Themes:	My story:
Genesis	Creation/ The Beginning Fall/Brokenness	
Exodus	Exit/Changes	
Leviticus	Wandering/ Following Christ	
Numbers	Holiness/ Redemption	
Deuteronomy	Reminders/ The Theme of Your Story	
	Prophecy/ Encouraging Others	

Creating Authentic Relationships

If I gave everything I have to the poor and even sacrificed my body, I could boast about it; but if I didn't love others, I would have gained nothing. Love is patient and kind. Love is not jealous or boastful or proud or rude. It does not demand its own way. It is not irritable, and it keeps no record of being wronged. It does not rejoice about injustice but rejoices whenever the truth wins out. Love never gives up, never loses faith, is always hopeful, and endures through every circumstance.

1 Corinthians 13:3-7

Friendship . . . is born at the moment when one . . . says to another: What! You too?
C. S. Lewis

Friendship is unnecessary, like philosophy, like art. . . . It has no survival value; rather it is one of those things that give value to survival.
C. S. Lewis

Day 1

If I gave everything I have to the poor and even sacrificed my body, I could boast about it; but if I didn't love others, I would have gained nothing. Love is patient and kind. Love is not jealous or boastful or proud or rude. It does not demand its own way. It is not irritable, and it keeps no record of being wronged. It does not rejoice about injustice but rejoices whenever the truth wins out. Love never gives up, never loses faith, is always hopeful, and endures through every circumstance.

1 Corinthians 13:3-7

The hard part of love and relationships is PEOPLE. And not just "those people" . . . I'm talking about ALL of us. We are all sinners, every last one of us! We all make mistakes. It's tempting to give up on friends who have let us down, but God's Word calls us to keep loving. When Christ was asked what the greatest commandment was, he replied, "'You must love the LORD your God with all your heart, all your soul, and all your mind.' This is the first and greatest commandment. A second is equally important: 'Love your neighbor as yourself'" (Matthew 22:37-39).

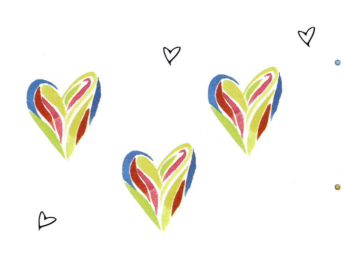

We are called to love ALL people as we would want to be loved. Even the people who are hard to like. Even the people who seem to have no interest in leaving their sin. We can truly love people who do not believe in the same things we do. We can be patient and kind, honoring others before ourselves and forgiving anyone who does us wrong. God will give us what it takes to do this!

The Scripture passage for today gives us a guide for how to live in love. In today's verses, highlight in one color what love is and in another color what love is not. Underline the words **always** and **never**, and circle the word **truth**. Did you notice that the word **truth** in the verses comes before any of the **always** and **nevers**? Authentic relationships are built on truth.

I hope and pray this chapter helps you navigate your friendships and see Jesus in the middle of both the joy and hurt!

PRAYER

Jesus, thank you for loving us and showing us what authentic love looks like. Help me to pursue relationships with people who believe your truths and to show your love to those who don't yet.

BIBLE JOURNAL

SUPPLY LIST

- butcher paper, kraft paper, or brown paper bag
- ruler
- scissors
- pencil
- pen or fine-point marker
- paint, markers, colored pencils, crayons, or anything else you want to color with
- paintbrush (if using paint)
- cup of water (if using paint)
- cardboard (you can use an old packing box or cereal box)
- glue

OVERVIEW

We have a long verse to memorize this week! Today you're going to make an accordion-folded Scripture booklet to help you memorize a little bit at a time.

STEPS

1. Cut a strip of kraft paper 3 inches wide and 20 inches long.
2. Measure 5 inches from the bottom of your paper strip and mark the spot very lightly with your pencil.
3. Take the bottom of your paper and fold it upward, making a crease at your pencil mark.
4. Turn your paper over and fold the folded section up to make another 5-inch-long folded section.
5. Continue turning and folding (like folding a paper fan) until your paper is folded into 4 sections.

6. Unfold your paper. With a pen or fine-point marker, write this week's verse on one side of the paper, a little bit in each folded section.
7. Decorate your paper however you like.
8. Cut your cardboard into 2 pieces, each 3 inches by 5 inches. You can decorate one side of each piece if you like.
9. Glue a piece of cardboard to the back of the first section of your paper (the side without writing).
10. Glue the other piece of cardboard to the back of the last section of your paper.
11. Once the glue has dried, open your verse booklet. Memorize the words you wrote on the first section. Once you have those down, move on to the next section, then the next, then the next!

Day 2

As iron sharpens iron, so a friend sharpens a friend.

Proverbs 27:17

Welcome to bestie day! Check out the first half of today's short-and-sweet verse:

_____

sharpens _____ .

    Sometimes it helps to think about what our verse doesn't say: it doesn't say "as iron sharpens ice cream" or even "as a rose petal sharpens a paintbrush." It's talking about a relationship between two similar and STRONG things—iron and iron, an even match.

    Let's look at a biblical example: Christ's friends. He had lots of acquaintances and followers, but then he had a solid group of only 12 friends (his disciples), and then three really close friends.

Jesus went with [his disciples] to the olive grove called Gethsemane, and he said, "Sit here while I go over there to pray." He took Peter and Zebedee's two sons, James and John, and he became anguished and distressed. He told them, "My soul is crushed with grief to the point of death. Stay here and keep watch with me."

Matthew 26:36-38

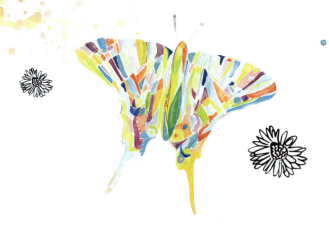

Circle Jesus' three besties in the verses you just read. These are the only three disciples Christ invited to pray with him when he knew he was being called to the cross. It's nice to have lots of friends, but when the stakes are high, we need to be choosy about who we depend on. While we are called to love everyone, our besties should be chosen wisely. They should be trustworthy people we can take advice from and pray with.

PRAYER

Lord, I pray for besties in my life who love you and your truth! I pray that you will give me wisdom for who to build close friendships with. And when I do find a close friend, I ask that you would make us like iron sharpening iron, pointing one another to you.

BIBLE JOURNAL

SUPPLY LIST

- sketchbook or piece of paper
- pencil
- markers or colored pencils
- pictures of doughnuts (optional)
- your imagination

OVERVIEW

Today we are thinking of and praying for all our friends!

STEPS

1. Make a list of your best buddies and write a few words that describe each of them. Say a little prayer for each one, thanking God for them and asking him to bless them.
2. Just for fun, we are going to draw each friend as a doughnut!
3. Look at the words you wrote by each of your friends' names and think, *What flavor would each of you be? Do you have sprinkles? Cream filling?* Draw your doughnut friends and color them with markers or colored pencils. You can look at pictures of doughnuts to help you out if you want.
4. For extra fun, create silly names for each doughnut friend, like "Sweet Sally" or "Cotton Candy Catherine."
5. If you have time, make some extra copies of your picture to give to your friends.

Day 3

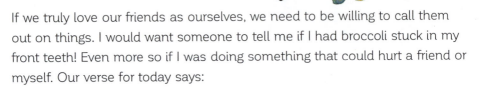

We will speak the truth in love, growing in every way more and more like Christ, who is the head of his body, the church.

Ephesians 4:15

If we truly love our friends as ourselves, we need to be willing to call them out on things. I would want someone to tell me if I had broccoli stuck in my front teeth! Even more so if I was doing something that could hurt a friend or myself. Our verse for today says:

We will speak the truth in _____.

This means we are not seeking to dishonor or shame others, or keep any record of their wrongdoing (see 1 Corinthians 13:5). Instead, we are to think of them before ourselves.

Don't be selfish; don't try to impress others. Be humble, thinking of others as better than yourselves.

Philippians 2:3

PRAY for your friend and about the situation before you speak. Ask God for the right words to show your love for your friend and to show you how to speak the truth in love into her life. We all like peace and harmony in our relationships, but "peace" without truth isn't really worth having. If truth is missing from your relationships, you might want to take a step back and think about what you really want those relationships to be like. Fight for friendships that are characterized by both truth and love. You can do it, friend!

PRAYER

Jesus, thank you for friendships that are founded on your truth! Please show me when and how to fight for real peace. And, Jesus, please help me to speak your truth in love.

WE WERE CREATED FOR **RELATIONSHIP.**

BIBLE JOURNAL

SUPPLY LIST

- sketchbook or piece of paper
- pencil
- markers or colored pencils
- Bible

OVERVIEW

Today we are making an illustration that will help us think about speaking the TRUTH in LOVE.

STEPS

1. Write the word **truth** in bubble letters in your sketchbook (see the Bubble Letters Art Note on page 42).
2. Create a different pattern in each letter.
3. Color your patterns with the markers or colored pencils.
4. Write the words from 1 Corinthians 13:4-7 around the word **truth**. Let the words of Scripture wrap around your bubble letters and spiral out to the edge of your paper.
5. Sit back and look at the truth wrapped in love.

Day 4

As long as Moses held up his hands, the Israelites were winning, but whenever he lowered his hands, the Amalekites were winning. When Moses' hands grew tired, they took a stone and put it under him and he sat on it. Aaron and Hur held his hands up—one on one side, one on the other—so that his hands remained steady till sunset.

Exodus 17:11-12, NIV

Ah! I love this! God was leading the Israelites into battle and commanded Moses to raise his staff. While it was raised, the Israelites won, but when Moses rested his arms, even for a moment, they began to lose. Moses was faithful, just tired.

According to our verses, who came to help Moses? _____ and _____

How cool is that? Moses' friends came alongside him and literally raised his arms for him. I can think of quite a few times I have needed my friends to come along and hold my arms up for me. The way people encourage me when I'm down or remind me of God's truths when I need them most shows God's love for me in such big ways.

SHARE YOUR STORY:
you never know who
or how it will
encourage others!

Here are three things to take note of before you go holding all your friends' arms up for them:

1. Moses and his friends were obeying God—Aaron and Hur weren't helping Moses do something sinful.
2. Aaron and Hur didn't do something for Moses that he should have been doing for himself—Moses was so tired that he had to have someone else come hold his arms up.
3. Aaron and Hur helped Moses in a way that wouldn't hurt themselves in the process.

Keeping these things in mind, ask God to show you whose arms might need a lift today.

Encourage one another, especially now that the day of his return is drawing near.
Hebrews 10:25

PRAYER
Jesus, help me to notice when my friends need help being obedient to your call; give me wisdom in knowing how and when to help them, and give me the courage to respond in love.

BIBLE JOURNAL

SUPPLY LIST

- piece of white paper
- white crayon or oil pastel
- watercolor paint (optional)
- paintbrush (optional)
- cup of water (optional)

OVERVIEW

Today we are going to pray for a friend who needs encouragement!

STEPS

1. PRAY about which of your friends needs encouragement today. (It's fine if you want to pick several!)
2. Write your friend a note in white crayon or white oil pastel on white paper. Remind your friend of God's truths, tell them what their friendship means to you, and encourage them to continue to seek God.
3. You can go ahead and watercolor over the crayon so it pops out, or tell your friend to paint over the paper to reveal your hidden message.

Day 5

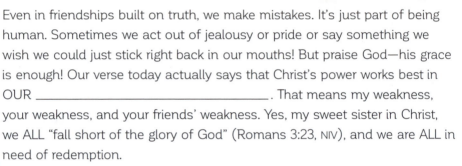

[God] said, "My grace is all you need. My power works best in weakness." So now I am glad to boast about my weaknesses, so that the power of Christ can work through me.

2 Corinthians 12:9

Even in friendships built on truth, we make mistakes. It's just part of being human. Sometimes we act out of jealousy or pride or say something we wish we could just stick right back in our mouths! But praise God—his grace is enough! Our verse today actually says that Christ's power works best in OUR _____. That means my weakness, your weakness, and your friends' weakness. Yes, my sweet sister in Christ, we ALL "fall short of the glory of God" (Romans 3:23, NIV), and we are ALL in need of redemption.

When we are weak, Christ is strong.

This is something you are going to have to preach to yourself: YES, God's grace is enough for THIS, and THIS, and THIS! When we trust God and his truth, revealed in the Bible, he gives us faith. Faith to trust that he is big enough and good enough to forgive us, even for whatever your THIS may be.

He is big enough and gives grace enough to forgive you and to help you forgive your friends.

Let us come boldly to the throne of our gracious God. There we will receive his mercy, and we will find grace to help us when we need it most.

Hebrews 4:16

PRAYER
Lord, give me humility to admit my mistakes and ask for forgiveness. I ask that you would show me grace when I mess up and help me to let that grace overflow into the lives of my friends.

REACH OUT IN FAITH!

BIBLE JOURNAL
weekend challenge

SUPPLY LIST

- canvas, poster board, or large piece of paper
- drop cloth or newspaper
- tube of acrylic paint (any color)
- black permanent marker
- watercolor paint
- paintbrush
- cup of water

OVERVIEW

This weekend we are going to watch our mess become something beautiful! This is something God loves to do in our lives.

STEPS

1. Lay your canvas out on a drop cloth or newspaper.
2. Splash, spray, or drop a blob of acrylic paint on your canvas. Let it dry.
3. Look at your mess and think of the most beautifully creative thing, person, or place you can make it into!
4. Add details and a background with the black permanent marker.
5. Paint in details with your watercolor paint so your blob stands out even in the end!
6. As you work, think of all the ways the Lord can make our messes into something beautiful.

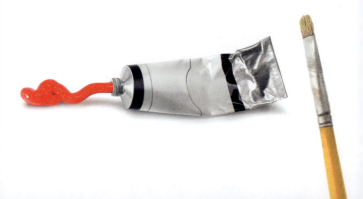

Art Medium: Any of various materials used to create a work of art.

Drawing Media: Pencil, ink, charcoal, etc.

Painting Media: Watercolor, oil, acrylic, etc.

Mixed Media: Using various art media together in one work of art.

ART NOTES

Seeking Our Creator

One thing I have asked of the LORD, that will I seek after: that I may dwell in the house of the LORD all the days of my life, to gaze upon the beauty of the LORD and to inquire in his temple.

Psalm 27:4, ESV

If I find in myself a desire which no experience in this world can satisfy, the most probable explanation is that I was made for another world.

C. S. Lewis

199

Day 1

> One thing I have asked of the Lord, that
> will I seek after: that I may dwell in the
> house of the Lord all the days of my life,
> to gaze upon the beauty of the Lord and to
> inquire in his temple.
> Psalm 27:4, ESV

Check out today's Scripture and underline all the active verbs: **asked**, **seek**, **dwell**, **gaze**, **inquire**. Now circle the words **one thing**.

Can you think of ONE THING you have asked of the Lord today? I wish I could say I have asked just to gaze upon his beauty . . . but my prayers more often go like this: "Jesus, help me with . . ." or "Lord, I really want . . ."

We know from God's Word that he wants to bless us:

> Take delight in the LORD, and he will give you the desires of your heart.
> Psalm 37:4, NIV

But does that mean God's going to just hand us whatever we want? I just saw this fabulous new romper online. I truly desire the romper; it is a desire of my heart. Is that what this verse is talking about?

Let's look at this from the Lord's perspective. What is he seeking? What is the greatest desire of his heart?

The LORD longs to be gracious to you.
Isaiah 30:18, NIV

The Lord longs to be gracious to _____ [fill in your name]. The desire of the Lord is to know YOU. Yup—let that soak in. The God of the universe wants to know YOU. His desire is for our hearts to reflect the verses we've been looking at: wanting to know him more, taking delight in him. He is able and willing to change our hearts. New rompers are fine, but they pale in comparison to knowing God, so let's start seeking him!

The world and its desires pass away, but whoever does the will of God lives forever.
1 John 2:17, NIV

PRAYER
Lord, I pray that you would be working in my heart and mind, calling me to seek after your desires. I pray that you would take the desires of this world out of my mind and replace them with the desire to know you more.

☐ get REAL
☐ dig DEEP
☐ CREATE!

BIBLE JOURNAL

SUPPLY LIST

- index card or piece of cardboard cut to index-card size
- plastic knife
- tube of acrylic paint (any color)
- toothpick or old pencil

OVERVIEW

Today's Scripture memory card will take a bit longer to write out than normal. As you shape each word, use the time to think about God's beauty and goodness.

STEPS

1. Use the plastic knife to spread a thick layer of paint on your card, like you're frosting a cake.
2. Use a toothpick or old pencil to carve the words of the verse into the paint.
3. Let the card dry overnight.

Day 2

[God] rescued them from their enemies.
Psalm 106:10

Enemies?! Remember our three enemies
that we talked about a few weeks ago? Read
these verses for a reminder of who and what they are. Circle each enemy
when you find it:

Stay alert! Watch out for your great enemy, the devil. He prowls around like a roaring lion, looking for someone to devour.
1 Peter 5:8

Do not love this world nor the things it offers you, for when you love the world, you do not have the love of the Father in you.
1 John 2:15

The heart is deceitful above all things and beyond cure.
Jeremiah 17:9, NIV

Wow! To seek the Lord, we have to fight all of these enemies on our own?! Not at all—our verse for today says God has already rescued us! And if we look further in Scripture, we find that God gives us weapons to fight them as well! Flip in your Bible to Ephesians 6:10-13 and fill in the blanks:

Therefore put on the full _____ of _____, so that when the day of evil comes, you may be able to stand your ground, and after you have done _____, to _____ (NIV).

When I feel overwhelmed and unsure of my next move, I remember the Israelites' battle in 2 Chronicles 20. Several different people groups came to attack them. The Israelites prayed, "We have no power to face this vast army that is attacking us." And then comes the best part!

We do not know what to do, but our eyes are on you.
2 Chronicles 20:12, NIV

How did the Lord respond?

The battle is not yours, but God's. . . . Do not be afraid; do not be discouraged. Go out to face them tomorrow, and the LORD will be with you.
2 Chronicles 20:15, 17, NIV

We can skip to the end of the Book (Revelation) and see that God wins. But God in his wisdom has you here today for a reason. Fight the good fight, sister!

PRAYER

Jesus, prepare my heart and mind to seek you and fight for a relationship with you. I ask that you would open my eyes to evil in this world and show me how to fight in a way that glorifies your name!

GOD WILL GUARD OUR MINDS!

BIBLE JOURNAL

SUPPLY LIST

· full-length mirror

· sketchbook or piece of paper

· pencil

· pictures of your favorite superhero

· markers, colored pencils, crayons, or anything else you want to color with

OVERVIEW

Who is your favorite superhero or book or movie character? I so wish I could shoot a bow and arrow like Katniss Everdeen! Today we are going to draw superhero self-portraits to remind us that we stand firm in God's strength!

STEPS

1. Look in the mirror and stand like a superhero. Maybe your hands are on your hips. Put those strong shoulders back!
2. Draw your face, arms, and legs, but leave your clothes lightly sketched in. Do your hero pose and look back in the mirror as often as you need to (see the Human Proportions Art Note for help).
3. Look at the pictures of your superhero and draw their uniform and weapons on your body—you can mix and match from different superheroes if you want!
4. Use your markers, colored pencils, or crayons to color your picture as you like.

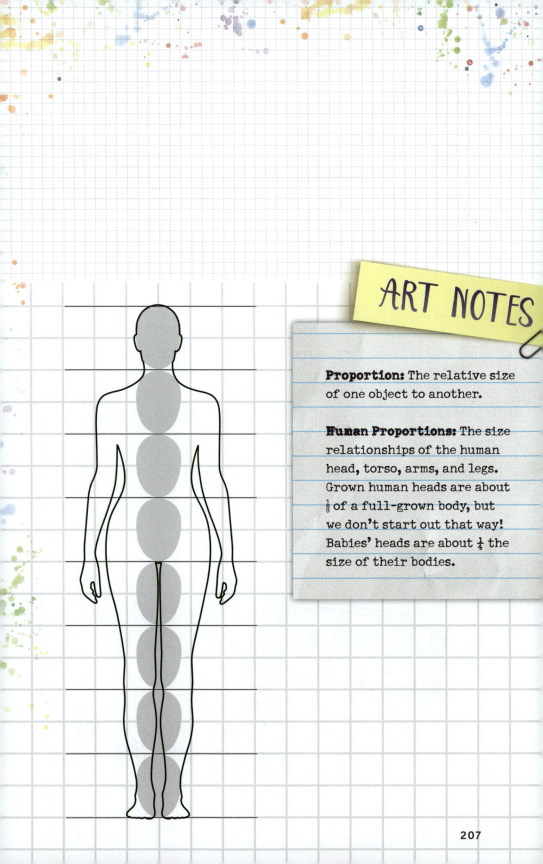

Proportion: The relative size of one object to another.

Human Proportions: The size relationships of the human head, torso, arms, and legs. Grown human heads are about $\frac{1}{8}$ of a full-grown body, but we don't start out that way! Babies' heads are about $\frac{1}{4}$ the size of their bodies.

Day 3

> As I looked at everything I had worked so hard to accomplish, it was all so meaningless—like chasing the wind. There was nothing really worthwhile anywhere.
>
> Ecclesiastes 2:11

Let's be honest, this verse, taken out of context, seems a little cray-cray, amiright?

To understand it better we need to look first at who the author is: King Solomon, son of King David (yup—David as in David and Goliath). When David died, Solomon became the king of Israel. God made Solomon an amazing offer: "What do you want? Ask, and I will give it to you!" (1 Kings 3:5). Solomon asked for wisdom, and God was so pleased that he gave Solomon not only wisdom but also riches and honor and a long life! (Solomon is also the guy who said, "Cut the baby in half," in 1 Kings 3:16-28—talk about cray-cray!)

Anyhoo, Solomon had seen a lot during his life, and God had given him wealth and wisdom. All his needs were provided for, and he was able

to enjoy his stuff. Make a list of all the things you would buy if God granted you great wealth today:

_____

_____

_____

_____

_____

Can we seek God with all this stuff? Can we seek God while we are seeking all this stuff? Look up 1 Corinthians 6:12. It says we have the right to do _____, BUT not everything is _____ . Solomon had access to anything and everything, but he learned that not everything is beneficial or good.

Take a moment today to consider what you are truly seeking and how that affects your relationship with God.

PRAYER

Jesus, thank you for creating this world full of fun things to do and have. Please walk with me today and show me how to give all the stuff in my life back to you!

BIBLE JOURNAL

- canvas, poster board, or large piece of paper
- paintbrush (the biggest one you have)
- watercolor paint
- cup of water
- pencil, pen, or fine-point marker
- drawing paper or scrapbooking paper
- glue
- acrylic paint

OVERVIEW

Let's create an abstract mixed-media piece to show all the different things we can have in our art!

STEPS

1. Choose your color scheme for your piece (see the Color Scheme Art Notes as well as the Color Family Art Note on page 42). If you have opposite color families in the background and foreground, it will create more contrast and highlight your focal point (see the Composition Art Note on page 9).
2. Take your watercolors and do some light washes all over your canvas. (Use a lot of water with just a little paint.) Let it dry.
3. Draw whatever you want on top of the watercolor with your pencil, pen, or fine-point marker. You can draw pictures, words, or just shapes and patterns.
4. Tear some pieces of drawing or scrapbooking paper and glue them onto your canvas. Let it dry.
5. Finish off with a few BIG brushstrokes of acrylic paint.

Monochromatic: A single hue (for example, red).

Color Scheme: A selection of colors according to certain rules.

Analogous: Colors next to each other on the color wheel (for example, red-orange, orange, and yellow-orange).

Complementary: Colors across from each other on the color wheel (for example, yellow and violet).

Split Complementary or Compound: Similar to complementary colors, but using a color and the two colors to either side of the color complementary to the first one (for example, green, red-orange, and red-violet).

Triad: Three hues evenly spaced on the color wheel (for example, green, violet, and yellow).

Day 4

Arise, shine, for your light has come,
and the glory of the LORD rises upon you.
Isaiah 60:1, NIV

Have you ever noticed how plants struggle to grow toward the light? I'm looking out my studio window right now and see a pink rose whose stem is twisted and crooked, but in a way that puts it directly above the hydrangea next to it. This little rose has been seeking the sun and is now basking in its light, above all the plants around it.

I look out and see the perfect illustration for this verse: Arise, shine, for your light has come!

This little rose has endured rainstorms, droughts, chipmunks, and tornadoes! It has been pruned in the autumn, rested in the winter, been rained on in the spring, and grown like crazy in the summer—all so it can shine like it does now!

Sometimes it's hard to seek God and see him in all the different seasons of life. Sometimes, I feel like I'm being cut back and refined too, and sometimes that's a hard place to be. But in each season, it is GOD who is at work in us. Go back and read the second part of today's verse. Circle the name of the person whose glory rises upon us. I pray that when it's your day to arise and shine, you will be ready! Ask him to prune, water, and shine on you!

PRAYER

Lord, I praise you for your light! I praise you for being my Gardener. I ask you, Lord, to continue to grow my faith today—whether that means pruning, resting, watering, or shining!

BIBLE JOURNAL

SUPPLY LIST

- sketchbook or piece of paper
- pencil
- mirror

OVERVIEW

Today you are going to think about the feelings that come with each of the four seasons of life and practice drawing the emotions you show on your beautiful face!

STEPS

1. Divide your paper into four sections either by folding it in quarters and then unfolding it or by drawing lines through the middle horizontally and vertically. Label the first section "pruning," the second "resting," the third "watering," and the fourth "shining."

2. Think about what it means for God to "prune" you—cutting bad stuff out of your life. How does that feel? Look in the mirror and practice facial expressions that show that emotion until you get one that looks right. (You might want to do this when no one else is around!)

3. Draw your face and expression in the "pruning" section of your paper. Remember to look in the mirror to draw—don't try to make up what you look like, or you will end up looking like a cartoon! You can also look at the Facial Proportions Art Note to help you get your facial proportions correct. Don't worry too much about detail today—just think about how you can communicate emotion with your drawings!

4. Repeat steps 2 and 3 for "resting" (waiting on God or finding peace and refreshment in him), "watering" (God giving you what you need to grow), and "shining" (showing God to others through your words and actions).

Facial Proportions:

Hairline

Eyes

Mouth

Ears

Self-Portrait: A likeness of oneself, usually focusing on the face.

Line of Symmetry:
The imaginary line where you could fold the image and have both halves match exactly.

Your eyelids cover part of your eye.

this   not this

The space between your eyes is equal to the width of one of your eyes.

Day 5

Follow my advice, my son; always treasure my commands. Obey my commands and live! Guard my instructions as you guard your own eyes. Tie them on your fingers as a reminder. Write them deep within your heart.

Proverbs 7:1-3

I want to offer a confession: I am disorganized. Can you relate? I mean, I try and try. I even got a supercute new planner this year, and I try to put all my appointments in my iPhone so it will *ding* when I need to be somewhere. But I still miss important things—sometimes I get distracted, and sometimes I accidentally set my reminder time to p.m. instead of a.m. (or a.m. instead of p.m.)!

The point of all of this is that I am in constant need of reminders. (Maybe I need an assistant!) And my walk with Jesus isn't too different. I need to be reminded to call on him, I need to be reminded that he is with me, and sometimes I need big, huge reminders that he loves me.

Rewrite the last line of the verse for today:

_____

_____

_____

_____

_____

For us to truly seek God, we must realize our weakness and remind ourselves of his goodness, faithfulness, and deep love for us. Scripture even tells us to write these truths on our hearts! God is faithful, but we even need him to remind us to seek him!

God gives us a great reminder in the last book of the Bible: "Remember, therefore, what you have received and heard; hold it fast, and repent" (Revelation 3:3, NIV). Ask him to write his truths on your heart today!

PRAYER

Jesus, thank you for being my salvation in all ways. I pray that you would remind me of your goodness and love for me when I need it most.

AGAIN...
HE has already done the work.

BIBLE JOURNAL
weekend challenge

- canvas, poster board, or large piece of paper
- pen or fine-point marker
- paintbrush (the biggest one you have)
- acrylic paint
- palette (you can also use a disposable plate or piece of cardboard)
- cup of water

OVERVIEW

This is a big one! We're going to make what artists call nonrepresentational art—art that doesn't copy a person, place, or thing from the real world. Instead, we'll be using colors and shapes to represent our feelings and thoughts.

STEPS

1. Choose one Scripture verse that has spoken to your heart this week and write it out with your pen or fine-point marker on the back of your canvas. Turn the canvas over.
2. What color does this verse make you think of most? Mix up your acrylic paint to make that color and paint a thick horizontal brushstroke across your canvas.
3. Mix other colors that the verse makes you think of. Maybe it's a verse about peace, so you use pastels. Maybe the verse is about anger or fighting and you use bold, dark colors. Maybe it's a combination of both!
4. Continue adding different brushstrokes until you feel like the verse is all on the canvas. Hang it in your room as a reminder of the verse it represents.

Trusting Our Creator

I am convinced that nothing can ever separate us from God's love. Neither death nor life, neither angels nor demons, neither our fears for today nor our worries about tomorrow—not even the powers of hell can separate us from God's love. No power in the sky above or in the earth below—indeed, nothing in all creation will ever be able to separate us from the love of God that is revealed in Christ Jesus our Lord.

Romans 8:38-39

I believe in Christianity as I believe that the Sun has risen, not only because I see it, but because by it I see everything else.

C. S. Lewis

Day 1

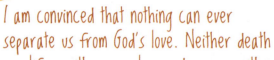

I am convinced that nothing can ever separate us from God's love. Neither death nor life, neither angels nor demons, neither our fears for today nor our worries about tomorrow—not even the powers of hell can separate us from God's love. No power in the sky above or in the earth below—indeed, nothing in all creation will ever be able to separate us from the love of God that is revealed in Christ Jesus our Lord.

Romans 8:38-39

NOTHING can ever separate us from the love of God! Praise him! But if that's true, why is it so hard for us to trust him? I mean, I trust that he came and died and rose again and can save me from my sins. But can I trust him with this book I am writing? Can I trust him with my new job? I don't think he teaches art, so maybe I'll have to do that part! Did Jesus ever take a math test? Can you trust him with the drama you're having with your friends or your family? Let's search the Scriptures for some help.

Turn in your Bible to Mark 9:17-24 and fill in these blanks:

One of the men in the crowd spoke up and said, "Teacher, I brought my son so you could _____ him. He is possessed by an _____ that won't let him talk. . . .
So I asked your disciples to cast out the evil spirit, but they couldn't do it. . . . Have mercy on us and help us, _____
_____ ."

"What do you mean, '_____
_____'?" Jesus asked. "Anything is
possible if a person _____."
The father instantly cried out, "I do believe,
but help me _____ my
_____!"

Mark 9:17-18, 22-24

Sometimes I am like this poor dad. I can't even imagine what it would be like to watch his own son go through so much suffering! His prayer hits home—"I do believe, but help me overcome my unbelief." I KNOW in my brain that I can trust God, but sometimes my heart struggles! I'm praying that today we can all learn to trust God a little more with our minds AND our hearts.

Trust in the LORD with all your heart; do not depend on your own understanding. Seek his will in all you do, and he will show you which path to take.

Proverbs 3:5-6

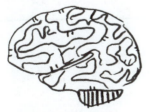

We are called to **THINK!**

(so...use your BRAIN!)

BIBLE JOURNAL

SUPPLY LIST

- 16 index cards
- drop cloth or newspaper
- permanent marker
- watercolor paint
- paintbrush
- cup of water

OVERVIEW

This week's verse is another long one! Today you're going to make a puzzle to help you memorize it.

STEPS

1. Lay out your index cards in four rows of four each (make a rectangle) on top of your drop cloth or newspaper.
2. With your permanent marker, write five or six words of the verse on each index card, starting in the top left corner of your rectangle.
3. Take your watercolors and paint a big, continuous design over the entire rectangle of index cards.
4. Once they're dry, scramble up the index cards and then see if you can put them back together in the right order. Do this several times every day to help you memorize the verse.

Watercolor Techniques:

Wash

Bleed

Dry Brush

225

Day 2

This is what the LORD says—he who created you, Jacob, he who formed you, Israel: "Do not fear, for I have redeemed you; I have summoned you by name; you are mine."

Isaiah 43:1, NIV

What is the Lord saying here? "I have summoned YOU,

_____ [fill in your name]; YOU are mine."

When you pass through the waters, I will be with you; and when you pass through the rivers, they will not sweep over you. When you walk through the fire, you will not be burned; the flames will not set you ablaze. For I am the LORD your God, the Holy One of Israel, your Savior.

Isaiah 43:2-3, NIV

God has placed us in a world he very well knows can cause us to fear and doubt. But he promises to go with us and to protect us. It's our choice whether to sweat the little (and big) stuff or trust him with it.

One of the best reasons to trust God is that we can only see what's right in front of us, while he can see the whole picture!

Now we see only a reflection as in a mirror; then we shall see face to face. Now I know in part; then I shall know fully, even as I am fully known.

1 Corinthians 13:12, NIV

Did you read that last nugget? We can trust God is doing what's best for us because he calls us by name, and he alone knows us FULLY.

Through him God created everything in the heavenly realms and on earth. He made the things we can see and the things we can't see.

Colossians 1:16

PRAYER
I praise you that you call me by name. I praise you that I am YOURS. Please hold my hand as I learn to trust you. I pray that you will continue to inspire awe in me of what is to come!

BIBLE JOURNAL

SUPPLY LIST

- Bible
- pencil
- sketchbook or piece of paper
- mirror

OVERVIEW

Today we are illustrating 1 Corinthians 13:12. We are going to think about seeing Christ!

STEPS

1. Look up Revelation 21 and read the whole chapter. (I know—it's a lot! Ask an adult or older sibling to read it with you if you need some help.)
2. If you're okay with marking in your Bible, underline descriptive words and circle things or people who will be in heaven.
3. Find a mirror and do a close-up drawing of your eye, looking carefully at the shapes in the reflection.
4. See how your eye reflects light? Instead of drawing what you actually see inside the reflection, draw what you think heaven will be like, based on Revelation 21.
5. For an extra challenge, try to use correct perspective (see the Perspective Art Note on page 65).

Day 3

You have not received a spirit that makes you fearful slaves. Instead, you received God's Spirit when he adopted you as his own children. Now we call him, "Abba, Father." For his Spirit joins with our spirit to affirm that we are God's children. And since we are his children, we are his heirs. In fact, together with Christ we are heirs of God's glory.

Romans 8:15-17

Another reason we can trust God is he is our perfect Father. The Bible says that God loves us so much that he has adopted us as his daughters! According to Oxford Living Dictionaries, **adopt** means "legally take another's child and bring it up as one's own." Yup, our GOOD God, the Creator of the entire universe, wants to bring us up as his own.

While our heavenly Father is ALL good, everyone on earth is only human. God is our spiritual Father, but he has entrusted for a time our very human earthly parents or guardians with our care. One of the Ten Commandments even says, "Honor your father and mother. Then you will live a long, full life in the land the LORD your God is giving you" (Exodus 20:12). While God has planned our relationship with our parents to be good

and loving, we know from God's Word that our enemy's goal is to deceive or take away what should be the very best for us (see John 10:10). If there are things that make you sad or mistrusting at home, don't be discouraged, but seek your heavenly Father and ask for help! Our heritage is with him, and he is worthy of our faith and trust! (If things are so bad that you don't feel safe, ask God to help you find an adult you can trust and talk to them about what's going on.)

PRAYER

Father, thank you for adopting me as your daughter! Thank you for sending your Son to earth to fight for my chance to live life to the fullest! Please help me cling to you and your truths as I seek to honor my earthly parents or guardians.

BIBLE JOURNAL

SUPPLY LIST

- collage materials (copies of photographs, printed pictures, newspaper, etc.)
- sketchbook or piece of paper
- glue
- paintbrush (optional)
- water (optional)
- small cup (optional)

OVERVIEW

Today, we are going to make a "broken beautiful" collage to help us remember how God can make beautiful things out of our mess. Art tip: put some glue and water in a small cup and use a paintbrush to collage with—this will make less mess and give you more control over the medium.

STEPS

1. Find collage materials that represent different parts of your life (school, church, family, activities, etc.). Make copies of anything you don't want to tear up and use those instead.
2. Tear your collage materials into pieces.
3. Think of how God created all of the things about your life for good, but because they are part of this world, they are broken. Arrange all your scraps into color-wheel order as well as you can (see the Color Wheel Art Note on page 56). Then start collaging them into a sign of redemption—the rainbow! Be creative! "I have placed my rainbow in the clouds. It is the sign of my covenant with you and with all the earth" (Genesis 9:13).

Day 4

Just say a simple, "Yes, I will," or "No, I won't." Anything beyond this is from the evil one.

Matthew 5:37

Between yes and no or black and white are "gray areas." The older you get, the more "gray areas" there seem to be in life. Gray areas aren't necessarily bad, but our verse today tells us that God doesn't want us to mess around in them when we're making promises. He wants us to simply say yes or no and stick to it—to be trustworthy like he is trustworthy.

Seek the Kingdom of God above all else, and live righteously, and he will give you everything you need.

Matthew 6:33

Before we make a promise in any situation, we should first seek the Lord in prayer and search his Word for guidance. A good next step is seeking wise advice from family and friends who share our dedication to Christ.

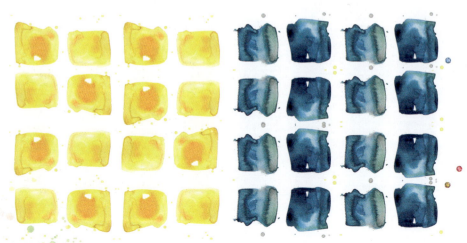

After we have followed these steps and given our promise, we need to trust God with the outcome. Sometimes even when we have sought the Lord, the outcome isn't what we expected. When we have given our yes or no, we are to stick to it! (The only exception would be if we discover that keeping a promise would mean doing something that goes against God's Word.)

So when a sibling or friend has asked you to join a sports team or be in a play with them, and you asked your parents, prayed about it, and told them you would, keep your promise and GO to practice! Likewise, if you promised your mom you would clean your room (this was a daily battle for me and my mom!), then do it! Trust God and his Word to give you what you need to see it through.

Not following through can allow shame and guilt in your life—and it can hurt people who are counting on you. So by all means, let your yes be yes and your no be no!

WE can NOT CHANGE OUR OWN ♡'s

BIBLE JOURNAL

SUPPLY LIST

- object to draw (something simple, like an egg)
- flashlight or other source of direct light
- sketchbook or two pieces of paper
- pencil
- blender or paper towel
- marker

OVERVIEW

Today we are going to draw some gray areas and practice VALUE and CONTRAST!

STEPS

1. Set up your object with your flashlight pointed right at it. Make sure you can see the light hit the object and the shadow cast to the side.
2. Open your sketchbook to a new page or grab a piece of paper and begin sketching with a pencil.
3. Draw the horizon (tabletop, most likely) and the object overlapping it.
4. Now use your pencil to add value to your object (see the Value Art Note on page 16 and the Contrast Art Note on page 119). Try to get as many different grays as you can—turn the pencil different ways and use your blender or paper towel to rub it in!
5. The last step on this page is to add a shadow. Look carefully—there is often more than one shadow to draw!
6. On another piece of paper, follow the same steps, but with ONLY a marker.
7. You cannot get gray areas with the marker. Keep your drawing simple.
8. Think about the contrast this drawing has between the white and the black—the yes and the no!

Trusting Our Creator

Day 5

In the same way, the Spirit helps us in our weakness. We do not know what we ought to pray for, but the Spirit himself intercedes for us through wordless groans.

Romans 8:26, NIV

So many times I sit down and don't know where to start writing. I type out a sentence and then delete, delete, delete. Try again, change some things, delete, delete, delete again. Sometimes it's because I get five new ideas while I am working on one. Other times I am simply uninspired—I just don't have anything to say! When I remember to step back and ask the Holy Spirit to guide my words, I literally pray that God would write this book for me! Because the truth is, it doesn't matter what I say—all that matters is what he says.

And "in the same way" that he meets me in my studio typing on my laptop, the Spirit helps YOU in your weakness. He meets you when you don't know what to ask for, when you have too many thoughts to get them all out, when you are uninspired or just not feeling it. How awesome is our God who

knows us so well that when we don't know what to say, "the Spirit himself intercedes for us through wordless groans."

Take a minute and practice your wordless groaning. Maybe shoot for something between a whale and a bullfrog—ha-ha!

But seriously, the Holy Spirit is bigger, more active in our lives, and more loving than we can understand. And "all he does is just and good, and all his commandments are trustworthy" (Psalm 111:7).

PRAYER

Lord, send your Spirit to intercede for me, to help me trust you when I don't know where to start or what to say. I praise you for being so big that you know all things, and so loving that you care about them.

RESULTS ARE NOT THE POINT OF PRAYER.

weekend challenge

SUPPLY LIST

- canvas, poster board, or large piece of paper
- markers
- paint
- paintbrush
- cup of water

OVERVIEW

This weekend we are going to focus on how to trust God even when we can't feel him with us. We are going to cover a canvas with moments from our lives and reflect on how God was and is at each point with us.

STEPS

1. Think of the entire canvas as your life.
2. Choose different-colored markers to represent different emotions—maybe yellow is joy, red is anger, blue is excitement, green is peace, etc.
3. Think of a memory, and make a dot on your canvas with the color that reminds you of how that memory makes you feel. Maybe you start at the top with a yellow dot for the day your little sister was born, or draw a blue dot for a first day of school or winning a game!
4. Fill the canvas with as many memory dots as you can.
5. Take a marker in a color you haven't used yet and start a line on one side of your canvas. Go through every single dot (let your line overlap itself as often as you like!) and end up going off the other side of the page.
6. Paint in all the different shapes made by the overlapping lines and think about all the ways your life overlaps with other people's lives.
7. Last, imagine that God is present in every inch of the canvas (your life). He is at the same time in every place, part of every connection, above, behind, and through it all.

Healing

By his wounds you are healed.
1 Peter 2:24

Look for yourself, and you will find in the long run only hatred, loneliness, despair, rage, ruin, and decay. But look for Christ and you will find Him, and with Him everything else thrown in.

C. S. Lewis

Day 1

By his wounds you are healed.
1 Peter 2:24

A very wise woman I know says, "Life is all about learning to recover." To me this feels like medicine for living in a fallen world, and it reminds me that we have HOPE. Because Christ came, died, and rose again, we can be healed!

Because we are human, there comes a point when our ability to help ourselves runs out. We need help from someone else. And the ultimate help has come in Christ.

By his wounds _____ [insert your name] is healed.

And through Christ's death on the cross, the Holy Spirit is able to offer us healing and help in all sorts of ways. One of these ways is through the people God puts in our lives.

I have this verse up in my kitchen so I can read it every day: "You must warn each other every day, while it is still 'today,' so that none of you will be deceived by sin and hardened against God" (Hebrews 3:13). An encouraging note from a friend or an impromptu prayer at school—there is something supernatural that can only be God that lifts us up in these places!

When we are aware of our enemies and our own shortcomings, we can see our need to come together. Look around you and encourage those who are drifting away, becoming angry, or giving in to fear. Let's help each other heal! Amen? Amen!

PRAYER

Jesus, I pray that you would help me realize when I need to heal and help me take time to do it. Give me wisdom to know which people in my life need your encouragement, today and every day.

BIBLE JOURNAL

SUPPLY LIST

- magazines, newspapers, or advertising mailers (ones you have permission to cut up)
- scissors
- index card
- glue

OVERVIEW

Today you're going to take cut-up words and put them together to make a whole. As you cut and paste, think about how God heals your wounds and makes them whole.

STEPS

1. Look through your magazines, newspapers, and ads to find each word in this week's verse. Cut the words out. Try to find them in different fonts and colors if you can (see the Font Art Note on page 21). If you can't find a word, you can cut out individual letters and put them together.
2. Glue the words in order on your index card.

Day 2

Enter through the narrow gate. For wide is the gate and broad is the road that leads to destruction, and many enter through it. But small is the gate and narrow the road that leads to life, and only a few find it.

Matthew 7:13-14, NIV

Often when I was growing up, I believed the lie that life would get easier if I just did [fill in the blank]. If I just didn't watch R-rated movies, if I was just more active in my youth group, if I could just be good enough. Then the road of life would open wide for me and everything would fall into place.

I couldn't have been further from the truth. Read the Scripture above again.

Underline all the times you read the word *gate*. There are two gates we can choose from—the wide gate that many enter through, and the narrow gate that Christ tells us to enter through, but that only a few find. What makes the path to the narrow gate so difficult?

Christ calls his beloved children to live for a higher purpose: "We don't look at the troubles we can see now; rather, we fix our gaze on things that cannot be seen. For the things we see now will soon be gone, but the things we cannot see will last forever" (2 Corinthians 4:18).

PRAYER

Jesus, I confess that I want to just do a few things and have the easy road rolled out for me. I confess that I have believed this as truth even though it is not in your Word. I praise you for setting me apart, and I ask that you guide me to the narrow gate—the gate to LIFE!

It's hard to focus on what is unseen—it takes prayer, discipline, and faith. It's easy to get sidetracked and lose sight of the narrow road.

So what happens if you go the wrong way? Mm-hmm . . . You STOP, change direction, and ask your Good Shepherd to lead you back. Sister, it's easy to get discouraged or feel ashamed when we should have known the way, but God is always waiting to bring us back to the right road. To stay or get back on the path we must learn to accept forgiveness, HEAL from our brokenness, and choose to move toward God again.

BIBLE JOURNAL

SUPPLY LIST

- sketchbook or piece of paper
- pencil
- permanent marker
- markers, colored pencils, crayons, or anything else you want to color with
- eraser

OVERVIEW

Today we are going to draw the two paths and gates as part of a maze!

STEPS

1. Start by writing **heaven** in the center of your page, pretty small.
2. Very lightly, with your pencil, begin drawing two maze paths starting at the same point: one that leads from the side of your paper to **heaven** and one that leads right off the other side of the page.
3. Add details to the path to heaven. It needs to be hard to find, rocky, and narrow—add lots of lines and obstacles.
4. Add details to the path that goes nowhere. This one can be wide and easy to follow!
5. Trace over your maze with a permanent marker and color it. Erase any pencil marks that still show.
6. When you are done, make some copies of your maze and see if your friends or siblings can make it through!

Day 3

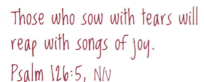

Those who sow with tears will reap with songs of joy.
Psalm 126:5, NIV

Have you heard the song "Blessings" by Laura Story? It's one of my all-time faves—if you haven't heard it before, ask your adult if you can look it up on YouTube now! My favorite line is from the chorus: "What if your blessings come through raindrops, what if your healing comes through tears?" It's a beautiful way to sing a really hard truth.

My human response to both of these is "Why?" Why can't we be healed through rainbows and sunshine, through smiles, on big, comfy couches? Doesn't that sound nicer? The truth is that we were created for another place—heaven. "In this tent we groan, longing to put on our heavenly dwelling" (2 Corinthians 5:2, ESV). But we are here, in our earthly "tent," where there's sick people, uncomfortable places and situations, fighting, and sin.

Read today's verse again. It is part of a song written for people to sing as they entered God's temple. They were preparing to be in the presence of the one true God who created them. Sounds a lot like the way we look forward to meeting God in heaven, doesn't it? Sometimes our healing looks like the

stories in the Bible, but sometimes it comes through tears and crying out to God. He hears you. He cares. And he will heal.

You keep track of all my sorrows. You have collected all my tears in your bottle. You have recorded each one in your book.

Psalm 56:8

Our present troubles are small and won't last very long. Yet they produce for us a glory that vastly outweighs them and will last forever!

2 Corinthians 4:17

PRAYER

Lord, help me see you in hard things. Help me to trust that you are working big plans for GOOD even in things that make me sad. And, Lord, please turn my tears into songs of JOY!

HE COLLECTS ALL OUR TEARS.

BIBLE JOURNAL

SUPPLY LIST

- sketchbook or piece of paper
- crayons, watercolor paint, and acrylic paint
- paintbrush
- cup of water
- plastic fork or knife
- gold leaf or gold sequins
- glue

OVERVIEW

We are going to illustrate the hope God brings in a dark season!

STEPS

1. Fill a sketchbook page or a piece of paper with cool and dark colors (see the Color Family Art Note on page 42). Try to use a variety of materials and marks. Maybe crayons, watercolor, and then a few large brushstrokes of acrylic paint on top?

2. Add texture with a plastic fork or knife—scrape some color off the page, and maybe spread some of it back on? Try to make it look like the wind is blowing all over the page.

3. Last, add a small speck of gold leaf (you can find this at your local craft store) or glue on a gold sequin. Gold leaf was used to identify saints in Byzantine art. It was often used to create a halo around a saint's head, but sometimes it covered the whole background! Think of your little speck of gold as a glimpse of Christ in the midst of a storm—Christ redeeming your tears with shouts of joy!

Day 4

How beautiful on the mountains are the feet of the messenger who brings good news, the good news of peace and salvation, the news that the God of Israel reigns!

Isaiah 52:7

The word **beautiful** brings to mind a painting, or a person, or a flower . . . but probably not someone's feet, right?!

You should clothe yourselves instead with the beauty that comes from within, the unfading beauty of a gentle and quiet spirit, which is so precious to God.

1 Peter 3:4

This verse says that outward beauty falls short of inward beauty—that the words we bring from deep within us, the words we hold dear to our hearts, are what make us beautiful; that our gentle and quiet spirits are _____ to God.

The story God is writing for each of us is our inward beauty. God is faithfully redeeming us and changing our lives, and so our stories or testimonies of his goodness have the power to change and heal hearts—even our own. You've already written out your story, so share it! Today, pray to be the feet of Jesus, bringing good news of peace and salvation to those around you!

PRAYER

Jesus, thank you for all the people you have placed in my life to share peace and remind me of your goodness when I need it most. I pray, Lord, that you would so fill me with your peace and goodness that it wouldn't have anywhere to go but to overflow into the lives of those around me!

BIBLE JOURNAL

SUPPLY LIST

- a shoe
- sketchbook or piece of paper
- pencil
- eraser

OVERVIEW

Today we are going to imagine our shoes sharing God's good news!

STEPS

1. Take your shoe off (yes, the shoe you are wearing right now!) and place it lengthwise on the table in front of you.
2. Grab a pencil and draw the shape of the outside of the shoe, then draw the big shapes inside.
3. Add the stitching and small designs. With your pencil, draw dots or checkerboard designs or whatever you see to add texture to your shoe (see the Texture Art Note on page 131).
4. Last, add the laces or straps—remember that laces are shapes, not just lines!
5. When you are done, write the verse from today around the outside of your drawing!

Day 5

Truly my soul finds rest in God; my salvation comes from him.
Psalm 62:1, NIV

Resting is one of the best ways we can help our mind and body heal. When I read the psalms, I am easily distracted because they seem to just repeat themselves. "Praise the Lord," "Rejoice," "Cry out to the Lord" over and over! But did you know the psalms were written as SONGS? When you can step back and read them like they were intended to be sung, they make a lot more sense. Think about the last song you listened to—most likely it had a chorus that repeated itself, just like the choruses found in many psalms.

Flip through the first five chapters of Psalms and look for the word *selah*. (It's often out to the right in italics.) How many did you find? _____

Have you ever paid attention to this word before? We're not sure exactly what *selah* means, but it is used to communicate a break in the singing, a pause, a time to reflect on what was just said, a time for people to respond to the Word of God.

Today, I want you to consider the rhythm of your life, just like in a song or a psalm—when are you able to rest and respond to the Lord? Take a minute to fill in the chart on the next page. Don't worry, no one is looking! So be honest with yourself.

What are you doing?	How are you resting?
Wake up	
Morning	
Lunchtime	
Afternoon	
Evening	
Night	
Bedtime	
Other	

Now go back and make sure you have time to "selah," or rest and respond, throughout your day. If you aren't taking time to rest with God, build time into your schedule! My favorite time is early in the morning or in the bath before bed.

Those who live in the shelter of the Most High will find rest in the shadow of the Almighty.
Psalm 91:1

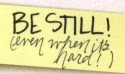
BE STILL!
(even when its hard!)

PRAYER
Jesus, thank you for creating me with purpose and energy, but also with the need to rest and rely on YOU. Thank you for meeting me in those times of rest and giving me fresh energy, joy, and patience!

BIBLE JOURNAL

SUPPLY LIST

- sunset or picture of one
- sketchbook or piece of paper
- oil pastels or crayons—with extra white ones for blending

OVERVIEW

REST, watching and drawing the sunset!

STEPS

1. Watch a sunset or find a picture of one. Maybe you have a photo handy from a special occasion?
2. Use your oil pastels to color in each color you see as the sunset fades from the sky.
3. Last, take your white oil pastels and carefully blend each color together. Think of the blending as the selahs between each part of the sunset.

Last Day

Daughter, your faith has made you well. Go in peace.

Mark 5:34

Faith that heals! Don't we all need a little of that?! I hope and pray your journey through *Made to Create with All My Heart and Soul* has excited your soul, revealed just how precious and special YOU are, and given you some truths and tools to walk out your faith!

The verse for today is about another special and precious daughter of our King. She was ill, but God had given her faith that he could heal her.

She had suffered a great deal from many doctors, and over the years she had spent everything she had to pay them, but she had gotten no better. In fact, she had gotten worse. She had heard about Jesus, so she came up behind him through the crowd and touched his robe. For she thought to herself, "If I can just touch his robe, I will be healed."

Mark 5:26-28

The next few verses say that Christ immediately healed her, and when he felt healing power go out from him, he looked for the woman and said, "Daughter, your faith has made you well. Go in peace" (Mark 5:34). How cool—she didn't even have to ask! God's healing power came when she reached out her hands in FAITH.

There are two truths for YOU from this story:

1. Following Jesus does not mean we are without conflict or struggle, just that we know who to run to for help and healing. "Lead me to the rock that is higher than I" (Psalm 61:2, NIV).
2. With just the tiniest amount of faith, we can be God's hands and feet. "I tell you the truth, if you had faith even as small as a mustard seed, you could say to this mountain, 'Move from here to there,' and it would move. Nothing would be impossible" (Matthew 17:20).

YOU, my dear friend, are truly CREATED FOR A PURPOSE and ready to walk in faith! Thank you for sharing this time with me.

By God's grace alone,
Lauren Duncan

You made all the delicate, inner parts of my body
    and knit me together in my mother's womb.
Thank you for making me so wonderfully complex!
Your workmanship is marvelous—how well I know it.
You watched me as I was being formed in utter seclusion,
    as I was woven together in the dark of the womb.
You saw me before I was born.
Every day of my life was recorded in your book.
Every moment was laid out
    before a single day had passed.
Psalm 139:13-16

FINAL CHALLENGE

Keep a prayer journal for the next year! Pick a book of the Bible and start reading. Find verses that speak to your heart and write them, draw them, paint them, and collage them! Write notes to God in your selah time. Record God's answers to your prayers. Date your pages so you can look back on God's faithfulness.

If you have trouble getting started, you can always use our CREATE acronym as a guide!

Calm your heart and listen to God's Word. Read a Scripture verse and change your spiritual posture.

Raise your hands in worship!

Examine your heart and tell the Lord what you need.

Ask the Lord for forgiveness and for help forgiving others.

Talk to God about what scares or concerns you and ask for protection.

Express what's on your heart!

About the Author

Lauren Duncan marvels at the big and bold circles God has made in her life. She was born and continues to reside in Auburn, Alabama. She has loved creating from an early age—her parents signed her up for art classes and bought her supplies to keep her busy.

Lauren got her undergraduate degree from Auburn University and her master's in art education from the University of Alabama at Birmingham. She taught art in Birmingham and later at an international Christian school in Ghana, West Africa. She returned to Auburn for what she thought would be a brief stay but met her husband and ended up making Auburn home again.

Currently, Lauren is an adjunct professor of art at Auburn University, teaches art to small groups, helps run her family store, and spends time in her studio. She prayerfully follows the Lord's nudges to paint, write, and love on sweet foster babies. It is her hope and prayer that her words and brush-strokes would help others along on their journey and inspire hope in the hearts they encounter.

Express Your Creativity

with these books for young writers and artists!